PLOTINUS
ENNEAD V.1

THE *ENNEADS* OF PLOTINUS
With Philosophical Commentaries

*Series Editors: John M. Dillon, Trinity College, Dublin
and Andrew Smith, University College, Dublin*

Also Available in the Series:

Ennead II.5: On What Is
Potentially and What Actually
by Cinzia Arruzza

Ennead IV.3–4.29: Problems
Concerning the Soul
by John M. Dillon and H. J.
Blumenthal

Ennead IV.4.30–45 & IV.5:
Problems Concerning the Soul
by Gary Gurtler

Ennead IV.8: On the Descent
of the Soul Into Bodies
by Barrie Fleet

Ennead V.5: That the Intelligi
are not External to Intelle
and on the Good
by Lloyd P. Gerson

Ennead VI.4 & VI.5:
On the Presence of Being,
One and the Same,
Everywhere as a Whole
by Eyjólfur Emilsson
and Steven Strange

Forthcoming Titles in the Series include:

Ennead I.1: What is the Living
Being, and What is Man?
by Gerard O'Daly

Ennead I.2: On Virtues
by Suzanne Stern-Gillet

Ennead I.6: On Beauty
by Andrew Smith

Ennead II.4: On Matter
by Anthony A. Long

Ennead II.9: Against the Gnostics
by Sebastian Ramon Philipp Gertz

Ennead III.7: On Eternity
and Time by László Bene

Ennead III.8: On Nature and
Contemplation
by George Karamanolis

Ennead IV.7: On the Immortality
of the Soul by Barrie Fleet

Ennead V.3: On the Knowing
Hypostases by Marie-Élise Zovko

Ennead V.8: On Intelligible Beauty
by Andrew Smith

Ennead VI.8: On Free Will
and the Will of the One
by Kevin Corrigan
and John D. Turner

PLOTINUS
ENNEAD V.1

On the Three Primary
Levels of Reality

Translation with an Introduction
and Commentary

ERIC D. PERL

PARMENIDES
PUBLISHING

Las Vegas | Zurich | Athens

PARMENIDES PUBLISHING
Las Vegas | Zurich | Athens

This edition published in 2015 by Parmenides Publishing
in the United States of America

ISBN soft cover: 978–1–930972–91–9
ISBN e-Book: 978–1–930972–92–6

Library of Congress Cataloging-in-Publication Data

Plotinus, author.
 [Ennead. V, 1. English]
 Ennead V.1 : on the three primary levels of reality? / Plotinus ; translation with an introduction and commentary Eric D. Perl.
    pages cm. -- (The Enneads of Plotinus with philosophical
commentaries)
 Includes bibliographical references and index.
 ISBN 978-1-930972-91-9 (soft cover : alk. paper) -- ISBN 978-1-930972-
92-6 (ebook)
 1. Soul. 2. Plotinus. Ennead. V, 1. I. Perl, Eric David, translator, writer
of introduction, writer of added commentary. II. Title. III. Title: On the
three primary levels of reality?
 B693.E52E5 2015d
 186'.4--dc23
                          2015030108

Author Photo by Jon Rou, Loyola Marymount University

Typeset in Warnock and Futura by Parmenides Publishing
Printed and lay-flat bound by Think Publications, Inc.,
El Dorado Hills, CA | www.thinkpublications.com

www.parmenides.com

Contents

To my parents

with love and gratitude

Introduction to the Series
With a Brief Outline of the Life and
Thought of Plotinus (205–270 CE)

Plotinus was born in 205 CE in Egypt of Greek-speaking parents. He attended the philosophical schools in Alexandria where he would have studied Plato (427–347 BCE), Aristotle (384–322 BCE), the Stoics and Epicureans as well as other Greek philosophical traditions. He began his serious philosophical education, however, relatively late in life, at the age of twenty-seven and was deeply impressed by the Platonist Ammonius Saccas about whom we, unfortunately, know very little, but with whom Plotinus studied for some eleven years. Even our knowledge of Plotinus' life is limited to what we can glean from Porphyry's introduction to his edition of his philosophical treatises, an account colored by Porphyry's own concerns. After completing his studies in Alexandria Plotinus attempted, by joining a military expedition of the Roman emperor Gordian III, to make contact with the

Brahmins in order to learn something of Indian thought. Unfortunately Gordian was defeated and killed (244). Plotinus somehow managed to extract himself and we next hear of him in Rome where he was able to set up a school of philosophy in the house of a high-ranking Roman lady by the name of Gemina. It is, perhaps, surprising that he had no formal contacts with the Platonic Academy in Athens, which was headed at the time by Longinus, but Longinus was familiar with his work, partly at least through Porphyry who had studied in Athens. The fact that it was Rome where Plotinus set up his school may be due to the originality of his philosophical activity and to his patrons. He clearly had some influential contacts, not least with the philhellenic emperor Gallienus (253–268), who may also have encouraged his later failed attempt to set up a civic community based on Platonic principles in a ruined city in Campania.

Plotinus' school was, like most ancient schools of philosophy, relatively small in scale, but did attract distinguished students from abroad and from the Roman upper classes. It included not only philosophers but also politicians and members of the medical profession who wished to lead the philosophical life. His most famous student was Porphyry (233–305) who, as a relative latecomer to the school, persuaded him to put into writing the results of his seminars. It is almost certain that we possess most, if not all, of his written output, which represents his mature thought, since he didn't commence writing until the age of forty-eight. The school seemingly had inner and outer circles, and Plotinus himself was clearly an inspiring and sympathetic teacher who took a deep interest in the philosophical and spiritual progress of his students. Porphyry tells us that when he was suffering from severe depression Plotinus straight away visited him in his lodgings to help him. His concern for others is also illustrated by the fact that he was entrusted with the personal education of many orphans and the care of their property and careers. The reconciliation of this worldly involvement with the encouragement to lead a life of contemplation is encapsulated in Porphyry's comment that "he was present to himself and others at the same time."

The *Enneads* of Plotinus is the edition of his treatises arranged by his pupil Porphyry who tried to put shape to the collection he had inherited by organizing it into six sets of nine treatises (hence the name *"Enneads")* that led the reader through the levels of Plotinus' universe, from the physical world to Soul, Intellect and, finally, to the highest principle, the One. Although Plotinus undoubtedly had a clearly structured metaphysical system by the time he began committing himself to expressing his thought in written form, the treatises themselves are not systematic expositions, but rather explorations of particular themes and issues raised in interpreting Plato and other philosophical texts read in the School. In fact, to achieve his neat arrangement Porphyry was sometimes driven even to dividing certain treatises (e.g., III.2–3; IV.3–5, and VI.4–5).

Although Plotinus' writings are not transcripts of his seminars, but are directed to the reader, they do, nevertheless, convey the sort of lively debate that he encouraged in his school. Frequently he takes for granted that a particular set of ideas is already familiar as having been treated in an earlier seminar that may or may not be found in the written text. For this reason it is useful for the reader to have some idea of the main philosophical principles of his system as they can be extracted from the *Enneads* as a whole.

Plotinus regarded himself as a faithful interpreter of Plato whose thought lies at the core of his entire project. But Plato's thought, whilst definitive, does according to Plotinus require careful exposition and clarification, often in the light of other thinkers such as Aristotle and the Stoics. It is because of this creative application of different traditions of ancient thought to the interpretation of Plato that Plotinus' version of Platonism became, partly through the medium of later Platonists such as Porphyry, Iamblichus (245–325), and Proclus (412–485), an influential source and way of reading both Plato and Aristotle in the Middle Ages, the Renaissance, and up to the early 19th century, when scholars first began to differentiate Plato and "Neoplatonism." His thought, too, provided early Christian theologians of the Latin and particularly of the Byzantine tradition, with a rich variety of metaphysical concepts with which to explore and express difficult doctrinal ideas. His fashioning of Plato's ideas into a consistent metaphysical structure, though no longer accepted as a uniquely valid way of approaching Plato, was influential in promoting the notion of metaphysical systems in early modern philosophy. More recently increasing interest has centered on his exploration of the self, levels of consciousness, and his expansion of discourse beyond the levels of normal ontology to the examination of what lies both above and beneath being. His thought continues to challenge us when confronted with the issue of man's nature and role in the universe and of the extent and limitations of human knowledge.

Whilst much of Plotinus' metaphysical structure is recognizably an interpretation of Plato it is an interpretation that is not always immediately obvious just because it is filtered through several centuries of developing Platonic thought, itself already overlaid with important concepts drawn from other schools. It is, nevertheless, useful as a starting point to see how Plotinus attempts to bring coherence to what he believed to be a comprehensive worldview expressed in the Platonic dialogues. The Platonic Forms are central. They become for him an intelligible universe that is the source and model of the physical universe. But aware of Aristotle's criticism of the Platonic Forms as lifeless causes he takes on board Aristotle's concept of god as a self-thinker to enable him to identify this intelligible universe as a divine Intellect that thinks itself as the Forms or Intelligibles. The doctrine of the Forms as the thoughts of god had already entered Platonism, but not as the rigorously argued identity that Plotinus proposed. Moreover the Intelligibles, since they are identical with Intellect, are themselves actively intellectual; they are intellects. Thus Plato's world of Forms has become a complex and dynamic intelligible universe in which unity and plurality, stability, and activity are reconciled.

Now although the divine Intellect is one it also embraces plurality, both because its thoughts, the Intelligibles, are many and because it may itself be analyzed into thinker and thought. Its unity demands a further principle, which is the cause of its unity. This principle, which is the cause of all unity and being but does not possess unity or being in itself, he calls the One, an interpretation of the Idea of the Good in Plato's *Republic* that is "beyond being" and that may be seen as the simple (hence "one") source of all reality. We thus have the first two of what subsequently became known as the three Hypostases, the One, Intellect, and Soul, the last of which acts as an intermediary between the intelligible and physical universes. This last Hypostasis takes on all the functions of transmitting form and life that may be found in Plato, although Plato himself does not always make such a clear distinction between soul and intellect. Thus the One is the ultimate source of all, including this universe, which is then prefigured in Intellect and transmitted through Soul to become manifest as our physical universe. Matter, which receives imperfectly this expression, is conceived not as an independently existing counter-principle, a dangerously dualist notion, but is in a sense itself a product of the One, a kind of non-being that, while being nothing specific in itself, nevertheless is not simply not there.

But this procession from an ultimate principle is balanced by a return movement at each level of reality that fully constitutes itself only when it turns back in contemplation of its producer. And so the whole of reality is a dynamic movement of procession and return, except for matter, which has no life of its own to make this return; it is inert. This movement of return, which may be traced back to the force of "love" in Plato or Aristotle's final cause, is characterized by Plotinus as a cognitive activity, a form of contemplation, weaker at each successive level, from Intellect through discursive reasoning to the merest image of rational order as expressed in the objects of the physical universe.

The human individual mirrors this structure to which we are all related at each level. For each of us has a body and soul, an intellect, and even something within us that relates to the One. While it is the nature of soul to give life to body, the higher aspect of our soul also has aspirations toward intellect, the true self, and even beyond. This urge to return corresponds to the cosmic movement of return. But the tension between soul's natural duty to body and its origins in the intelligible can be, for the individual, a source of fracture and alienation in which the soul becomes over-involved and overwhelmed by the body and so estranged from its true self. Plotinus encourages us to make the return or ascent, but at the same time attempts to resolve the conflict of duties by reconciling the two-fold nature of soul as life-giving and contemplative.

This is the general framework within which important traditional philosophical issues are encountered, discussed and resolved, but always in a spirit of inquiry and ongoing debate. Issues are frequently encountered in several different contexts, each angle providing a different insight. The nature of the soul and its relationship to the body is examined at length (IV) using the Aristotelian distinctions of levels of soul (vegetative, growth, sensitive, rational) whilst maintaining the immortal nature of the transcendent soul in Platonic terms. The active nature of the soul in sense-perception is maintained to preserve the principle that incorporeals cannot be affected by corporeal reality. A vigorous discussion (VI.4 and 5) on the general nature of the relationship of incorporeals to body explores in every detail and in great depth the way in which incorporeals act on body. A universe that is the product of design is reconciled with the freedom of the individual. And, not least, the time-bound nature of the physical universe and human reason is grounded in the life of Intellect, which subsists in eternity. Sometimes, however, Plotinus seems to break outside the framework of traditional metaphysics: the nature of matter and the One, each as non-being, though in a different sense, strains the terminology and structure of traditional ontology; and the attempt to reconcile the role of the individual soul within the traditional Platonic distinction of transcendent and immanent reality leads to a novel exploration of the nature of the self, the "I."

It is this restless urge for exploration and inquiry that lends to the treatises of Plotinus their philosophical vitality. Whilst presenting us with a rich and complexly coherent system, he constantly engages us in philosophical inquiry. In this way each treatise presents us with new ideas and fresh challenges. And, for Plotinus, every philosophical engagement is not just a mental exercise but also contributes to the rediscovery of the self and our reintegration with the source of all being, the Platonic aim of "becoming like god."

While Plotinus, like Plato, always wishes to engage his audience to reflect for themselves, his treatises are not easy reading, partly no doubt because his own audience was already familiar with many of his basic ideas and, more importantly, had been exposed in his seminars to critical readings of philosophical texts that have not survived to our day. Another problem is that the treatises do not lay out his thought in a systematic way but take up specific issues, although always the whole system may be discerned in the background. Sometimes, too, the exact flow of thought is difficult to follow because of an often condensed mode of expression.

Because we are convinced that Plotinus has something to say to us today, we have launched this series of translations and commentaries as a means of opening up the text to readers with an interest in grappling with the philosophical issues revealed by an encounter with Plotinus' own words and arguments. Each volume will contain a new translation, careful summaries of the arguments and structure of the treatise, and a philosophical commentary that will aim to throw light on the philosophical meaning and import of the text.

John M. Dillon
Andrew Smith

Abbreviations

DK   Hermann Diels and Walther Kranz, eds. *Die Fragmente der Vorsokratike*r. 7th ed. Berlin: Weidmannsche, 1954.

HS₁   P. Henry and H.-R. Schwyzer, eds. *Plotini Opera* I–III (editio maior). Paris and Leiden: Desclée de Brouwer and Brill, 1951–1973.

HS₂   P. Henry and H.-R. Schwyzer, eds. *Plotini Opera* I–III (editio minor, with revised text). Oxford: Oxford University Press, 1964–1982.

LSJ   H. G. Liddell and R. Scott. *A Greek-English Lexicon*. 9th ed. Revised by H. Jones. Oxford: Oxford University Press, 1940.

Smyth Herbert Weyr Smyth. *Greek Grammar*. Revised by Gordon M. Messing. Cambridge, MA: Harvard University Press, 1956.

SVF   J. von Arnim, ed. *Stoicorum Veterum Fragmenta*. Stuttgart: Teubner, 1968.

VP   *Vita Plotini* = Porphyry's *Life of Plotinus*, printed at start of HS1, HS2, MacKenna, and Armstrong.

Acknowledgments

I would like to thank the series editors, John M. Dillon and Andrew Smith, for giving me the opportunity to take part in this project and for their helpful suggestions; and the Bellarmine College of Liberal Arts at Loyola Marymount University, for a 2014 Summer Research Grant supporting the completion of the volume.

Introduction to the Treatise

Ennead V.1, numbered 10 in Porphyry's chronological listing and thus one of Plotinus' earlier works, bears the title *Peri tōn triōn archikōn hypostaseōn,* "On the Three Principial Hypostases," here translated, "On the Three Primary Levels of Reality." But Porphyry reports that Plotinus did not give titles to his writings, and that the titles he records, which have since become traditional, are "those that prevailed" (VP 4, 16–19). In the case of V.1, the traditional title is exceptionally misleading, in two ways. First, this title presents the treatise as if it were an exercise in theoretical metaphysics, aimed at distinguishing and describing soul, intellect, and the One as three ontological principles superior to the sensible world. Much of the work is indeed occupied with this theme. But the central topic of the treatise is in fact the self, and the metaphysical analysis takes place within this personal and spiritual context.

Like several of Plotinus' other early works (I.6 [1]; V.9 [5]; IV.8 [6]; VI.9 [9]), the treatise is primarily concerned with the ascent of the soul and is protreptic in nature, aimed at awakening the human soul to its alienation from itself and its divine origin and exhorting us to turn back and discover the higher levels of reality within ourselves. The "three hypostases," soul, intellect, and the One, are not an objectified scale of metaphysical entities to be climbed by a self which is extrinsic to them and which remains untransformed as it ascends. Rather, in ascending to intellect we become intellect (see, e.g., V.3.4, 10–12; V.8.10, 35–41); in ascending to the One we ourselves become "beyond reality" (VI.9.11, 41–42). Thus the "hypostases" are at once metaphysical principles and, in Pierre Hadot's excellent phrase, "levels of the self" (1993, 27): intellect is both the intelligible paradigm of the cosmos and the highest level of consciousness, and the One is both the source of all reality and the inmost center of the self. The present treatise is a particularly striking example of how, as is always the case in Plotinus, metaphysics is spirituality and spirituality is metaphysics.

The second way in which the traditional title is misleading is that the phrase "three hypostases" (a phrase that nowhere occurs in the work of Plotinus himself) tends to suggest that we are dealing with three different realities additional to one another, as if the One were a first thing, which generates intellect as a second thing, which in turn generates soul as a third thing. But Plotinus is at pains in the treatise to show that this is not the case. Rather, the relation of soul to intellect, and of intellect to the One, is in each case that of "image" (*eikōn* or *eidōlon*) and "expression" (*logos*), and the "generation" in question is nothing but the derivation of an image from its original. An image of something—for instance, a reflection—is not another, additional thing. It is, rather, the same thing at a secondary and inferior level of presentation. Thus Plotinus explains that the three levels are distinguished from one another only by their different modes of possession of the same content. This is the meaning of the important expressions, "nothing between but difference" (3, 21–22) and "separated only by difference" (6, 53), which he uses to describe the relation of soul to intellect and of intellect to the One. The principle that is operative throughout the sequence, and which is indeed a dominant theme of this treatise, is what will later become the scholastic maxim, "Whatever is received is received according to the mode of the recipient," or, as Plotinus expresses it elsewhere, "What is present must be understood to be present for the capacity of that which receives" (VI.4.11, 3–4). Thus Plotinus explains in Chapters 3 and 4 that soul is consti- tuted as soul, distinct from and subordinate to intellect, in that it possesses discursively and sequentially that which is found all together at once in intellect. This principle becomes especially prominent in Plotinus' discussion of the derivation of intellect from the One in Chapters 5–7. Confronted with the age-old problem of how a multiplicity, such as intellect, can derive from that which is free of all multiplicity, he explains that intellect is constituted as intellect, distinct from and subordinate to the One, in virtue of its own pluralizing mode of receiving that which occurs absolutely without differentiation in and as the One. Thus the "three hypostases" are not a series of beings additional to one another, but rather three levels of possession of the same content, and precisely as such are levels at once of reality and of the self. To ascend from soul to intellect to the One is not to pass from one world or set of objects to another, but to apprehend the same content in ever-greater concentration.

The movement of thought in this treatise is sufficiently straightforward. Plotinus begins with a vivid description of the human soul's neglect and ignorance of its own true nature and divine origin (Chapter 1). Chapter 2 is aimed at persuading the soul of its superiority to the body and of the divinity that it shares with the world-soul and the souls of the celestial bodies. Chapter 3 takes the ascent a step further by demonstrating the superiority of intellect to soul, and Chapter 4 continues this theme by expounding the greatness of intellect, its eternal possession of and unity with the whole of intelligible reality. Chapters 5 through 7 complete the ascent by showing that intellect, since it is multiple, cannot be the highest, but depends on and in that sense derives from the One, which is thus the supreme first principle of all reality. Chapters 8 and 9 are a doxographic excursus aimed primarily at showing that this doctrine is not an innovation but is the authentic teaching of Plato, with roots extending back to Pythagoras and a number of Presocratic philosophers. In Chapters 10 through 12 Plotinus returns to the issue of the self, showing that these transcendent levels are always present within us and urging us to discover them by turning our attention inward, away from sensible things and toward "the voices from above."

More, perhaps, than any other single treatise, V.1 can be read as a self-contained survey of Plotinus' system as a whole and hence to some degree as an introduction to his philosophy. Here he not only offers a summary account of all the levels of reality in relation to one another, but also presents in condensed form, often in as little as a single sentence or even less, an extraordinary number of themes to which he elsewhere devotes extended discussion or even entire treatises. These include the relation of the individual soul to the world-soul and to soul in general (IV.3, IV.9); the problem of the multiple self (I.1); the immortality of soul (IV.7); the undivided omnipresence of soul and intellect to the sensible, and the related principle of reception according to the capacity of the recipient (VI.4–5); eternity and time (III.7); the unity-in-duality of intellect and the intelligible (V.3, V.5, V.6,

V.9); the unity-in-multiplicity of the forms (V.8, V.9); the "Platonic categories" (VI.2); the nature of number (VI.6); the indeterminate dyad or "the matter in intelligibles" (II.4); how intellect derives from the One (III.8, V.2, V.3, V.4, V.5, VI.7); and the self-constitutive reversion of the lower level to the higher (V.3, VI.7). Incidentally, the presence of all these ideas in this early treatise, in terms which are wholly consonant with their full deployment elsewhere, serves to show how little actual development there is in Plotinus' thought over the course of his writings. However, because these themes are addressed here in extreme brevity, with highly compressed and elliptical argumentation, the treatise is far from self-explanatory and is very difficult to understand correctly unless the reader is already familiar with Plotinus. It is constantly in need of unpacking and of supplementation from other treatises where the same topics are addressed more fully, and this I have endeavored to provide in the Commentary. But taken together with such explanation and expansion, the treatise offers an excellent overview and introduction to the thought of Plotinus as a whole.

Treatise V.1 also holds a unique place in the history of Plotinus' influence on later thought, due to the special attention it has received from Christian readers both in antiquity and in the present. The theme of the "three hypostases," all of which are transcendent to the sensible cosmos; the characterization of each of them, albeit in different senses, as *theos*, "god"; and the description of the second hypostasis, intellect, as the *logos* of the first, have led Christian thinkers to find here a parallel to their own doctrine of the Trinity (cf. Brunner 1973, 86). But this was and is a profound misreading: the One, intellect, and soul are not all "god" in anything like the sense in which, in Christian theology, the three Persons of the Trinity are each and all the same God. On the contrary, Plotinus is concerned to stress the ontological posteriority and subordination of soul to intellect and of intellect to the One, which alone is the absolute first principle of all. The assimilation of Plotinus' "three hypostases" to the Christian Trinity thus represents a severe distortion or misunderstanding of one or both doctrines. In the domain of spirituality, however, the treatise's emphasis on interiority, the discovery of divinity within the soul as the inmost dimension of the self, has been taken up into Christian thought in a far more authentic way.

No doubt because of its nature as a survey, and also due to the special place it has historically held in relation to Christian thought, more discussion and commentary have been devoted to this treatise than to many other individual works of Plotinus. I have had constant recourse to Michael Atkinson's detailed commentary (1983), Fernand Brunner's insightful essay (1973), and, for the exceptionally difficult Chapter 7, Jesús Igal's close, line-by-line study (1971). For both translation and interpretation, I have consulted Fronterotta's French, Harder's German, and Igal's Spanish translations, as well as MacKenna's and Atkinson's English translations, and, above all, the splendid English translation by Armstrong in the Loeb Classical Library.

Note on the Text

Line numbers in the translation are approximate and do not always match the original Greek text. Since the commentary follows the sequence of the English translation, there may sometimes be a slight discrepancy in the ordering.

The Greek text adopted is that of the Oxford edition (taking into account the Addenda ad Textum in vol. 3, 304–325). Deviations from the text are noted in the commentary. Each *Ennead* is referred to by Roman numerals, followed by the number of the treatise, the chapter of the treatise, and, finally, separated by a comma, the line number or numbers, e.g, V.1.3, 24–27.

It is customary to add the chronological number given by Porphyry in his *Life of Plotinus* (*Vita Plotini*), so that, for example, V.1 is designated V.1 [10]. In this series the chronological number is given only where it is of significance for Plotinus' philosophical stance. The following chart indicates the chronological order.

Chronological Order of the *Enneads*

Enn.		Enn.		Enn.		Enn.		Enn.		Enn.	
I.1	53	II.1	40	III.1	3	IV.1	21	V.1	10	VI.1	42
I.2	19	II.2	14	III.2	47	IV.2	4	V.2	11	VI.2	43
I.3	20	II.3	52	III.3	48	IV.3	27	V.3	49	VI.3	44
I.4	46	II.4	12	III.4	15	IV.4	28	V.4	7	VI.4	22
I.5	36	II.5	25	III.5	50	IV.5	29	V.5	32	VI.5	23
I.6	1	II.6	17	III.6	26	IV.6	41	V.6	24	VI.6	34
I.7	54	II.7	37	III.7	45	IV.7	2	V.7	18	VI.7	38
I.8	51	II.8	35	III.8	30	IV.8	6	V.8	31	VI.8	39
I.9	16	II.9	33	III.9	13	IV.9	8	V.9	5	VI.9	9

	Enn.		Enn.		Enn.		Enn.		Enn.		Enn.
1	I.6	10	V.1	19	I.2	28	IV.4	37	II.7	46	I.4
2	IV.7	11	V.2	20	I.3	29	IV.5	38	VI.7	47	III.2
3	III.1	12	II.4	21	IV.1	30	III.8	39	VI.8	48	III.3
4	IV.2	13	III.9	22	VI.4	31	V.8	40	II.1	49	V.3
5	V.9	14	II.2	23	VI.5	32	V.5	41	IV.6	50	III.5
6	IV.8	15	III.4	24	V.6	33	II.9	42	VI.1	51	I.8
7	V.4	16	I.9	25	II.5	34	VI.6	43	VI.2	52	II.3
8	IV.9	17	II.6	26	III.6	35	II.8	44	VI.3	53	I.1
9	VI.9	18	V.7	27	IV.3	36	I.5	45	III.7	54	I.7

Synopsis

Chapter 1—*The fallen condition of the soul*

1–22 The soul becomes ignorant of itself and its divine origin by directing its attention and admiration to lesser, outward things.

22–35 To be turned back, the soul must be shown the contemptibility of the things it now admires, and reminded of its own true nature; the latter kind of discussion will be pursued here.

Chapter 2—*The greatness of soul*

1–27 Soul gives life, being, and value to the entire cosmos.

27–40 Soul animates the cosmos without being divided into mutually extrinsic parts.

40–50 Since soul is what makes the visible gods to be gods, soul itself is a higher god; our soul, considered in its purity, is of the same kind and worthy of the same honor.

Chapter 3—*Intellect is even greater and more divine than soul*

1–5 Exhortation to ascend from soul to intellect.

5–12 Soul is an image or outward expression of intellect.

12–25 Soul's reasoning is actualized by its possessing in its own way what it sees in intellect. Thus soul is posterior and intellect is prior and superior.

Chapter 4—*The nature of intellect*

1–16 Intellect encompasses in itself all reality, and so has no need to change, increase, or acquire anything.

17–25 Hence intellect is all things eternally, without sequence or temporal extension.

26–33 Intellect and being establish one another and coincide, constituting a unity-in-duality.

33–43 Deduction of the "Platonic categories": being, difference, sameness, motion, and rest are found throughout intellect.

Chapter 5—*Intellect is posterior to the One*

1–9 As a determinate multiplicity, or number, intellect is posterior to "the simple," from which it receives determination. *Qua* receptive, it is the indeterminate dyad.

10–13 Sensible magnitudes are posterior to intelligible reality, or number.

13–19 As number, intellect may be reduced to the indeterminate dyad, as that which receives determination, and the One, from which it receives determination.

Chapter 6—The derivation of intellect from the One

1–12 How does intellect come from the One? Let us extend ourselves in prayer to him.

12–27 The generation of intellect must involve no motion on the part of the One.

27–39 The metaphor of emanation helps us to conceive such generation.

39–53 Intellect is an expression of the One as soul is of intellect.

Chapter 7

1–18 Intellect constitutes itself as a multiplicity by possessing in its own, differentiated mode what is without differentiation in and as the One.

18–26 If the One were in any way determinate, it would be one of the beings, rather than the principle of all beings. Being is being in virtue of determination.

27–49 Review of conclusions: Intellect derives from the first principle, and generates the forms as its own contents; it generates soul as a subordinate image of itself.

Chapter 8—*Doxographic excursus*

1–14 These doctrines are not innovations, but can be found in Plato.

14–23 Parmenides, too, recognized the identity of intellect and being, and denied bodily motion to it; but he erred in regarding it as purely one.

23–27 The Parmenides in Plato's dialogue of that name speaks more accurately, distinguishing the three natures.

Chapter 9

1–7 Adumbrations of the doctrine of the One can be found in Anaxagoras, Heraclitus, and Empedocles.

7–27 Criticism of Aristotle's theories of intellect as the first principle and of a multiplicity of such principles.

28–32 Those of the ancients who most closely followed Pythagoras addressed the One.

Chapter 10—*Discovery of soul, intellect, and the One within ourselves*

1–10 These three are in us, as dimensions of the self that transcend the sensible.

10–31 The soul *qua* rational is the first level of the self that transcends the body.

Chapter 11

1–7 Since our soul is capable of reasoning, intellect must be in us as the enabling condition for such reasoning.

7–15 Hence the One must be in us, as the principle of intellect.

Chapter 12—*Why we are unaware of these possessions*

1–12 The One, intellect, and rational soul are always present and active in us; but we do not apprehend them because we are the whole soul, including the part which is oriented toward sensibles.

12–21 To apprehend these higher levels within ourselves, we must turn our attention to them, disregarding the sensible as far as possible.

Translation of
Plotinus Ennead *V.1 [10]*

On the Three Primary Levels of Reality

1. Whatever is it, then, that has made souls be oblivious of their father god, and, although they are portions from there and altogether his, be ignorant of both themselves and him? The principle of badness for them is audacity and becoming and the first otherness | and willing to 5 belong to themselves. Since they appeared to delight in independence and indulged extensively in being moved by themselves, running in the opposite direction and getting very far away, they were ignorant that they themselves are from there; just as children immediately torn from their parents | and brought up far away for a long time are 10 ignorant of both themselves and their parents. No longer, then, seeing him or themselves, scorning themselves

through ignorance of their race, honoring other things and admiring all things rather than themselves, and astonished and wondering at them and dependent on these things,

15 | they broke themselves away as far as possible from the things they turned away from in scorn. Thus it comes about that their honor for these [lesser] things and scorn for themselves is the cause of their complete ignorance of him. For that which pursues and admires something else at the same time confesses itself to be inferior; but making

20 itself inferior to things that come into being | and pass away, considering itself more contemptible and mortal than the things it honors, it could never lay to heart the nature or the power of god.

Hence two kinds of discourse are necessary for those who are in such a condition, if one is to turn them back to the things that are opposite and primary and lead them

25 up to what is highest | and one and first. What then is each kind? One, which we address fully elsewhere, is to show the contemptibility of the things that are now honored by the soul; the other is to teach and remind the soul what kind of race and worth it has. This is prior to the other, and when it is made clear will make the other

30 evident as well. This is what we must speak about now; | for it is close to what is being sought for and contributes to the other. For that which is seeking is the soul, and it ought to know what it is that is seeking, so that it may first come to know itself: whether it has the ability to

seek such [higher] things, whether it has an eye of such
a kind as to see them, whether it is appropriate for it to
seek them. For if they are alien, what is the use? But if | 35
they are akin, it is appropriate [to seek them] and possible to find [them].

2. Let all soul, then, first consider this well: that [soul] itself
made all living things, breathing life into them: those that
the earth nourishes, those that the sea [nourishes], those
in the air, those in the sky, the divine stars; it [made] the
sun, it [made] this great | universe and made it a cosmos;   5
it moves it around in order, being a nature other than the
things it orders and moves and makes live. And it must
be more honorable than these, for they come into being
and perish when soul departs from them or provides them
with life, but [soul] itself always is since it does not "depart
from itself."[1] | Its way of providing life, in the [universe   10
as a] whole and in particular things, is to be considered
thus. Let another soul—no small one, one that has become
worthy to look by being delivered from deception and from
the things that have bewitched other souls, one standing
firm in quietude—look at the great soul. Let | not only the   15
body that lies around it and the surging waves of the body
be quiet, but also all that surrounds it: the earth quiet,
the sea and air quiet, and the greater sky itself. And from

---

1   Plato, *Phaedrus* 245c8.

everywhere, into this universe at rest, let it conceive soul
as if flowing in from outside and pouring in and entering
20   from everywhere and illuminating it. | As sunbeams light
up a dark cloud and make it shine, giving it a golden look,
so soul, coming to the body of the universe, gave it life
and gave it immortality and awakened that which lay still.
And the universe, moved with an everlasting motion by
the wise guidance of soul, became a blessed living thing,
25   and came to have | value in virtue of the indwelling soul;
before soul it was a dead body, earth and water, or rather
the darkness of matter and non-being and "what the gods
abhor,"[2] as someone says.

The power and nature of [soul] may become more
evident and clearer if one thinks here of how it encom-
30   passes and drives the universe by | its own counsels. For
to all that magnitude, as far as it extends, [soul] has given
itself, and every interval both great and small is ensouled.
One body lies in one place and one in another, one is here,
another there, and some are in opposite positions, others
35   are separated from each other in other ways. | But soul
is not like that, and does not make things live by being
cut up into a part of itself for each one, but all things live
by the whole [soul], and all [soul] is present everywhere,
made like to the father who generated it with regard to
unity and ubiquity. And the universe which is multiple,

---

2   Homer, *Iliad* 20.65.

having one part here and another there, is one by [soul's] | power, and through [soul] this cosmos is a god. And the sun is a god because it is ensouled, and the other stars, and we ourselves, if anything [is a god] at all, for this reason; for "corpses are more to be thrown away than dung."[3] But that which causes the gods to be gods must be a god senior to them. But our [soul] is of the same kind, and when | you look at it without accretions, taking it purified, you will find the same honorable thing that we said soul was, more honorable than all that is bodily. For "all things are earth";[4] and even if they are fire, what [but soul] would be its burning? And the same goes for the things composed of these, even if you add to them water and air. But if a thing is to be pursued because it is ensouled, why | disregard oneself and pursue something else? If you admire soul in something else, admire yourself.

3. Since the soul is so honorable and divine a possession, trusting now that by such a means you will approach god, on such a basis ascend toward him. You do not have far to shoot at all: there are not "many things in between."[5] Grasp, then, what is | more divine than this divine thing, the upper region that neighbors soul, what soul is posterior to and comes from. For although [soul] is such a thing as

40

45

50

5

---

3   Heraclitus, DK B 96.

4   Aristotle, *Metaphysics* 1.8.989a9.

5   Homer, *Iliad* 1.156.

our account has shown, it is an image of intellect. As a
word in utterance is the expression of [the word] in soul,
so too [soul] is the expression of intellect and its whole
activity and the life which it sends forth for the existence

10 of another; | as fire has the heat that is with it and that
which it gives off. We must understand there [in the intel-
ligible] one activity that does not flow out but remains
in it, and one activity that exists as something else [viz.,
soul]. Since it comes from intellect, [soul] is intellectual,
and its intellect consists in reasonings; and its perfection,
again, is from [intellect], as from a father who raises what

15 he engendered, which was not perfect | in comparison to
himself. The existence of [soul], then, comes from intellect,
and its reason is made actual by intellect's being seen. For
when it looks at intellect, it possesses within itself and as its
own what it thinks and effects. And only these should we
call activities of soul, the ones [that it does] intellectually,
the ones that are proper to it; the inferior ones are from

20 elsewhere and are affects of such a soul. | Intellect, then,
makes [soul] still more divine both by being its father and
by being present to it. For there is nothing between but
their being different: one of course as subsequent and as
the recipient, the other as form. But even the matter of
intellect is beautiful, in that it is intellective and simple.
And how great intellect is, is clear from this very [point],

25 that it is superior | to soul, which is itself so great.

4. But one might also see this from the following: If one
marvels at this sensible cosmos, looking at its magnitude
and beauty and the order of its everlasting motion, and
the gods in it, some of whom are seen and others invis-
ible, | and the spirits, and all animals and plants, let him,   5
ascending to its archetype, to what is more true, behold
there all things intelligible and eternal with it in its own
awareness and life, and chief of these the undefiled intellect and immense wisdom, and what is truly the life "in
the age of Cronus,"[6] the god | who is fullness and intel-   10
lect. For it encompasses in itself all things immortal,
every intellect, every god, every soul, ever at rest. For why
seek to change when all is well? And where might it go,
when it has all things present to itself? Nor does it seek
to increase, since it is most perfect. Wherefore all things
in it are perfect as well, so that it may be altogether | per-   15
fect, having nothing which is not so, having nothing in
it that it does not think; and it thinks not by seeking but
by having. And its blessedness is not an acquisition, but
it is all things in eternity, and is the real eternity, which
time imitates, running around soul, passing from some
things and attending to others. For at [the level of] soul
[there is] one thing after another, | now Socrates, now a   20
horse, always some one among beings; but intellect is all
things. Hence intellect has in itself all things at rest and

---

6   Hesiod, *Works and Days*, 111.

is only, and the "is" is always, and nowhere future, for it
is "then" too; or past, for nothing there has passed away;
25 but all things are always steadfast | in that they are the
same, as if content with themselves because they are so.

Each of them is intellect and being and the whole
together is all intellect and all being: intellect, by thinking,
establishes being, and being, by being thought, gives to
intellect thinking and existence. But the cause of thinking is something else, which is also [the cause] for being;
30 thus | something else is the cause of both simultaneously.
For they are simultaneous and exist together and do not
depart from each other, but this one is two beings, at
once intellect and being, both thinking and that which
is thought: intellect as thinking and being as that which
is thought. For there could not be thinking unless there
35 is difference and also sameness. Thus intellect becomes |
these first: being, difference, sameness. But we must also
include motion and rest: motion, if it thinks, and rest, so
that [it may be] the same. And we must include difference,
so that there may be that which thinks and that which is
thought: if you take away difference, it becomes one and
will be silent; and also the things that are thought must
40 be different in relation to each other. | But we must also
include sameness, since it is one with itself, and there
is some unity common to all; and "the distinction is

difference."[7] The multiplicity of these produces number and quantity, and the particularity of each of these produces quality; and from these as principles come the others.

5. This god beyond soul, then, is multiple; and it is possible for [soul] to be among these things, conjoined with them, if it does not will to desert. Having drawn near and as it were become one with him, [the soul] asks, "Who is it, then, that generated this?" The simple, he who is prior to such multiplicity, | the cause of its being and its   5
being many, he who makes number. For number is not first. For in fact, unity is prior to the dyad and the dyad is second, and coming into being from unity has it as what determines it. [The dyad] is indeterminate in itself, but when it is determined, then it is number, number in the sense of reality; and soul is a number. | For masses and   10
magnitudes are not primary; for these thick things, which sensation considers beings, are posterior. And again, in seeds, it is not the moisture that is honorable, but what is not seen, and this is number and rational principle. So what is there [in the intelligible] called number and the dyad are rational principle and intellect. The dyad, understood as, so to speak, the substratum, is indeterminate; | but the number that comes from it and unity is each a   15
form, intellect as it were being shaped by the forms that

---

7   Aristotle, *Metaphysics* 4.2.1004a21.

have come to be in it. It is shaped in one way by the One but in another by itself, like vision in act; for intellection is sight which sees and both are one.

6. How, then, and whom, does it see? And how did it come into existence at all and come to be from him, so that it does see? For the soul now grasps the necessity that these things be, but further longs for what was repeatedly discussed also by the wise men of old: how, from a unity

5   which is such | as we say the One is, did anything whatsoever come to have existence, whether a multiplicity or a dyad or a number? Yet that did not remain by itself, but such a multiplicity flowed out as is seen among beings, and which we think fit to refer back to that. In this way, then, let us speak, calling upon god himself, not in audible

10   speech | but in soul extending ourselves in prayer to him, able in this way to pray alone to the alone.

Since, then, he is by himself as it were within the temple, remaining quiet beyond all things, the beholder must behold the things that are as it were the statues already

15   standing outside, or rather the statue that | appeared first, appearing in this way. For everything that moves, there must be something toward which it moves. Since there is none for that, we must not assert that it moves, but if something comes into being posterior to it, it must be generated while that is always turned toward itself.

20   (Generation in time must be set aside | when we are

discussing eternal beings, attributing to them in our discussion the generation that pertains to them, that of cause and order.) What comes to be from there, then, must be said to come to be without its being moved; for if something came to be by its being moved, what came to be would become third from that, after the motion, | and   25 not second. If, then, there is a second after it, this must come to exist while it is unmoved, neither inclining nor willing nor moving in any way at all. How, then, and what must we think is around that as it abides? An illumination from it, from it as it abides, like the sun's brightness, as | if it were running around it, always generated from it   30 while it abides. And all beings, while they abide, give off from their own being, around themselves on the outside, from the power present in them, a necessary dependent existence, which is an image, as it were, of the archetypes from which it emerged. Fire gives off heat from itself, | 35 and snow does not only keep cold within itself. Fragrant things, especially, bear witness to this; for as long as they exist, something around them proceeds from them, and what is nearby enjoys their existence. And all things, once they are perfect, generate; but what is eternally perfect eternally generates and generates what is eternal; and it generates what is lesser than itself.

What then must we say about | the most perfect?   40 Nothing comes from it except the greatest things after it. And the greatest thing after it, and the second, is intellect;

for intellect sees him and needs him alone, but he has no need of [intellect]. And that which is generated from what is greater than intellect is intellect, and intellect is greater than all things, because the other things are posterior to

45 it; | and such a thing is soul, an expression and activity of intellect, just as [intellect] is of him. But the expression [at the level] of soul is dim, for it is an image of intellect and so must look to intellect, and likewise intellect toward him, so that it may be intellect. But it sees him without being separated, because it is next after him and there is nothing between, as there is nothing [between] soul and

50 intellect. | Everything yearns for that which generated it, and loves this, and especially when that which generates and that which is generated are alone; but when that which generates is the most good, [that which is generated] is necessarily with him, as it is separated only by difference.

7. But we say that intellect is an image of that; for we must speak more clearly. First, we must say that what is generated must in a way be that and preserve much of it and be a likeness to it, as light is of the sun.

5   — But that is not | intellect. How then does it gener-ate intellect?

    — In that by its return toward it, it sees; and the seeing itself is intellect. For that which apprehends something else is either sense or intellect. [Consider] sense a line, etc.[8]

_____

8   This incomplete sentence appears to mean, "Consider sense as a line, intellect as a circle, the One as the center." See Commentary 7, 6–8.

— But the circle is such as to be divided, whereas this [the center] is not so.

— Here too there is a one; but the One is the power | of all things. The things, then, of which it is the power, 10 are what intellection beholds, as it were cutting them off from the power; otherwise it would not be intellect. For, of itself, it already has as it were an awareness of its power, that it is able to produce reality—for by itself, it even determines being for itself by the power that comes from that—and that reality is, as it were, | some one part 15 of the things that belong to that and come from that; and it is strengthened by that and is perfected into reality by that and from that. It sees that living and thinking and all things come to it from there, as to the divided from the undivided, because he is none of all things. For this is how all things are from him, because | he is not confined 20 by any shape; for that is one only, and if it were all things, it would be included among the beings. For this reason, that is none of the things in intellect, but all things are from it. This indeed is why they are realities: because they are already determinate and each has, as it were, a shape. Being must not float, as it were, in indeterminacy, | but must be fixed by determination and rest; and rest 25 in intelligibles is definition and shape, and by these it possesses existence.

"Of this lineage"[9] is this intellect, [a lineage] worthy
of the most pure intellect: to spring from none other than
the first principle, and once it has come to be, to generate
30 all beings with itself, all the | beauty of the forms, all the
intelligible gods. It is full of the things that it generated
and, as it were, swallows them up again by holding them
in itself, not letting them fall out into matter or be brought
up with Rhea: as the mysteries and the myths about the
gods say riddlingly that Cronus, the wisest god, before
35 generating Zeus, holds back what he generates | in himself,
and thus is full and intellect in satiety; and after that, they
say, he generates Zeus once he is full. For intellect generates soul when it is perfect intellect. For being perfect it
had to generate and not be sterile, since it is so great a
power. But here again, that which is generated could not
40 be greater, | but must be lesser than it, being an image,
and, by the same token is indeterminate, but determined
and, as it were, given form by that which generated [it].
And the offspring of intellect is a rational principle and
an existence, that which thinks discursively; and this is
what moves around intellect and is a light and trace of
45 intellect and dependent on that, on one side | joined to
that and thus filled from it and enjoying and partaking of
it and thinking, but on the other side in contact with the
things that are posterior to it, or rather itself generating

9   Homer, *Iliad* 6.211, 20.241; Plato, *Republic* 547a4–5.

things that are necessarily inferior to soul; these must be discussed later. And this is as far as divine things go.

8. And this explains why, for Plato, all things are three-fold "around the king of all"—he is speaking about the primary things—and "second around second things and third around third things."[10] And he also says that there is a "father of the cause,"[11] | meaning by "cause," intellect;   5 for his demiurge is intellect, and this he says makes soul in that "mixing-bowl."[12] But the "father" of the cause which is intellect he calls the Good, both beyond intellect and "beyond reality."[13] And he frequently refers to being and intellect as form. So Plato knew that intellect is from the Good, | and soul from intellect. These accounts given here,   10 then, are not new or of the present, but were said of old, though not openly; but the present theories are exposi-tions of them, relying on the writings of Plato himself as evidence that these doctrines are ancient. | Indeed,   15 Parmenides too, earlier, touched on such a doctrine in that he brought together being and intellect into identity, and did not place being among sensible things, saying, "Thinking and being are the same."[14] And he said that this

---

10   Plato, *Letter* 2, 312e1–4.
11   Plato, *Letter* 6, 323d4
12   Plato, *Timaeus* 41d4.
13   Plato, *Republic* 509b9.
14   Parmenides, DK B 3.

is unmoved: even though he attributed thinking to it, he
20 removed all bodily motion from | it so that it might stay
the same, and likened it to the mass of a sphere because it
possesses all things encompassed within it, and because
it thinks not outside but within itself. But he is at fault
for saying, in his own writings, that it is one, because
this "one" was found to be many. But the Parmenides in
25 Plato, speaking more accurately, distinguishes | from each
other the first One, which is more properly one, and the
second, which he calls "one-many,"[15] and the third, [which
he calls] "one and many."[16] And so he too is in agreement
as regards the three natures.

9. Anaxagoras, too, calling intellect pure and unmixed,
posits the first and separate, the One, but fails in precision
on account of his antiquity. And Heraclitus knows that
the One is eternal and intelligible; for bodies are always
5 coming into being | and "flowing." And for Empedocles,
strife divides but love is the One, and he too [takes] this
to be incorporeal, and [takes] the elements as matter.

    Aristotle, later, takes the first to be separate, and
intelligible; but by saying that it thinks itself,[17] going
back again, he makes it not first. And in affirming many
10 other intelligibles, | as many as the celestial spheres so

---

15 Plato, *Parmenides* 144e5.

16 Plato, *Parmenides* 155e5.

17 Cf. Aristotle, *Metaphysics* 12.7.1072b20; 12.9.1074b34.

that each may move one, he speaks with regard to the
intelligibles in a different way from Plato, positing what
is reasonable but does not possess necessity. But one
might doubt whether it is even reasonable; for it is more
reasonable that all the spheres, together making up one
system, look to one [principle], the first. | One might   15
inquire whether, for [Aristotle], the many intelligibles
come from one [principle], the first, or whether there are
many principles among the intelligibles. And if they come
from one, clearly this will be analogous to the way the
spheres are among sensibles, one encompassing another
and one, the outermost, ruling; so that there [among the
intelligibles] too the first would encompass the others,
and there will be | an intelligible world-order. And just as   20
here [in the sensible], the spheres are not empty, but the
first is full of stars and the others have stars, so too, there
[in the intelligible], the movers will have many things in
themselves, the truer things there. But if each [mover] is a
principle, the principles will be random; and why will they
be together and in agreement for one work, the | harmony   25
of the whole universe? And how can the sensible things
in the heavens be equal [in number] to the intelligibles,
the movers? And how can [the movers] be many in this
way, since there is no matter to separate them?

Thus, those of the ancients who most closely lined up
with the positions of Pythagoras and his followers, and of
Pherecydes, were | concerned with this nature; but some   30

worked this out fully in their own writings, while others
did not set it out in writings but in unwritten discussions,
or left it alone altogether.

10. It has now been shown that we must acknowledge
that this is the way things are: there is the One beyond
being, which is such as our argument intended to show,
as far as it was possible to demonstrate concerning these
matters; and there is, next, being and intellect; and third,

5   the nature of soul. | And just as in nature there are these
three aforesaid, so we must acknowledge these also in
ourselves. I mean, not in [ourselves as] sensible things—
for these [three] are separate—but above these, outside
of sensible things, "outside" in the same sense that these
things are "outside" the whole universe; so also, in the

10   things that pertain to man, | [I mean] the sort of thing
that Plato calls "the inner man."[18]

 Our soul, then, is something divine and of another
nature [than sensible things], as is all the nature of soul;
and it is perfect in possessing intellect. There is intellect
that reasons, and [intellect] that provides reasoning.

15   Now, that in the soul which reasons, needing no | bodily
organ for reasoning but possessing its activity in purity
so that it may reason purely, is separate and not mixed
with body; one would not go wrong in setting this in the

---

18 Plato, *Republic* 587a7.

first intelligible. For we must not seek for a place where we will establish it, but must make it outside all place. For thus it is | by itself and outside and immaterial, when it is   20
alone, having nothing from the nature of body. This is why [Plato] says with regard to the whole [universe] that [the demiurge] "then" cast the soul around it "from outside,"[19] indicating that [aspect] of the soul which remains in the intelligible; and with regard to us he said obscurely that it is "on top," in the head.[20] And his exhortation to | be   25
separate is not meant spatially, for this is separated by nature, but with regard to inclination and imaginations and the estrangement from the body, if somehow one could lead up even the remaining aspect of soul and bring along to what is higher that [aspect] of it which is established here [below], which alone is | the craftsman and shaper   30
of the body and has concern with it.

11. Since, then, there is soul that reasons about just and beautiful things, and reasoning that inquires whether this is just or that is beautiful, there must also be some stable justice, from which there comes to be reasoning at [the level of] soul. Or how else could it reason? And | if soul   5
sometimes reasons about these things and sometimes does not, there must be in us intellect, which does not reason discursively but always possesses justice; and there

---

19 Plato, *Timaeus* 34b4, 36e3.
20 Cf. Plato, *Timaeus* 90a5.

must be the principle and cause and god of intellect. Not
being divided, he remains, and as he does not remain in
place, he must, again, be contemplated in many things,
10 in each | of those that are able to receive him, as other; as
the center [of a circle] is in itself, but each of [the parts] in
the circle has a point in it, and the radii bring to this what
is proper to each. For by such a thing in us we too touch
15 and are with and depend on it; and we | who converge
thither are established there.

12. How then, since we possess such great things, do we
not apprehend them, but are for the most part idle with
regard to such activities, and some do not exercise them
at all? They are always engaged in their own activities,
5   intellect and what is prior to intellect, always in itself, and |
soul, the "ever-moving," is in this state. For not everything
which is in soul is already perceptible, but it reaches us
when it enters into perception. But when each active thing
does not communicate with what is perceptive, it has not
yet pervaded the whole soul. Hence we do not yet know,
because we are [involved] with what is sensitive and are not
10 a portion | of soul but the whole soul. And further, each
aspect of soul, since it is always living, always exercises
by itself its own activity; but recognition occurs when
there is communication and apprehension. It is necessary, then, if there is to be apprehension of the things that
are thus present, to turn that which apprehends inward,

and pay | attention to what is there. Just as, if someone   15
waiting for a voice that he wants to hear, turning away
from other voices, should arouse his ear toward the best
of things heard, when it comes; so too, here, dismissing
sensible sounds except as far as necessary, we must keep
the soul's power of apprehension | pure and ready to hear   20
the voices from above.

Commentary

Chapter 1

The treatise opens with a discussion of the human soul's failure to recognize its own true nature and the divine principles from which it derives. In attending to and locating its good in outward, sensible things, subject to generation and corruption, the soul is alienated from itself and its "father god." In order to be converted, the soul must be reminded of its true nature and origin.

1, 1–2 *Whatever is it ... their father god*: The term *epilathesthai*, here translated "be oblivious," is an allusion to Plato's myth of the soul's pre-existence and prior knowledge of intelligible reality, its forgetting this knowledge at birth, and its need to recollect what it previously knew (*Meno*

81a5–86c2; *Phaedo* 72e3–77a5; *Phaedrus* 246d6–249c4).
But neither in Plato nor in Plotinus should this be taken
literally, as an involuntary forgetting of the soul's temporally prior experience. It is rather a mythic expression
of the soul's latent, neglected possession of intelligible
reality within itself, and its need to direct its attention
to this reality. On this point in Plato see Dorter (1972,
215–17); Perl (2014, 47–52). The etymological connec-
tion of English "latent," from Latin *latere*, "to lie hidden,
go unnoticed," with Greek *lēthē/lanthanō/epilathesthai*,
is worth noting here. The central theme of the present
treatise is that the soul's badness consists in its directing
its attention (*prosochē*: 12, 15) "outward" and "downward"
to sensible things rather than "inward" and "upward" to
the higher principles that are within it. As Chapter 12,
above all, makes clear, this is not literally a forgetting of
the soul's past experience, but rather a failure to attend
to what we always possess, and the primary purpose of
the treatise is to exhort us to re-direct our attention to
the higher principles that are present but disregarded
within ourselves. Hence the term "oblivious," connoting
"unaware because inattentive," conveys the sense better
than the more common translation "forget." See LSJ, s.v.
epilēthēs, which gives meanings for *epilanthanomai* that
include "let a thing escape one," "lose thought of," and
"leave disregarded, neglect."

It is unclear whether the phrase "father god" refers to intellect, the One, or, vaguely, to both together as the higher principles from which souls derive. In the present treatise, where Plotinus is concerned with the precise hierarchical relations among soul, intellect, and the One, he refers to intellect as the "father" of soul (2, 38) and the One as the "father" of intellect (8, 4; see also 6, 50–52). But elsewhere he speaks of the One as the "father" of the soul (e.g., VI.9.9, 35–38). The question is not of the first importance, since in the immediate context Plotinus is simply observing that the soul has its origin in a divinity superior to itself.

To translate this phrase as "their father, God" (as does, e.g., Armstrong), is misleading. *Theos* in non-Christian Greek is not a proper noun but an appellative. To call something *theos* is not to name a person but to say what sort of thing it is: Socrates is a man, Bucephalus is a horse, Zeus is a god. Plotinus' meaning is that the soul has a divine origin, not that its father is a person named "God." "Their divine father," though less literal, might convey the sense better.

1, 2 *portions from there*: Plotinus' point is not that souls are "pieces" broken off, as it were, from a greater whole, but that by nature they belong to and are members of the divine. "In this passage, *moiras* should not suggest corporeal division: Plotinus means that the soul has issued forth from the spiritual divine world" (Brunner 1973, 62–63). Here as elsewhere, Plotinus alternates freely between personal and spatial terms for the soul's divine source and destination; see below, 3, 6, where he refers to intellect as soul's "upper neighboring region," and 6, 23, where "from there" (*ekeithen*) refers to the One. "There" is of course not a place, but a higher level at once of reality and of the self.

1, 3 *ignorant of themselves and him*: The failure to recognize the higher, divine levels of reality is also a failure to recognize the higher, divine levels of the self. Throughout the Platonic tradition, self-knowledge and knowledge of true reality are inseparable. In taking the sensible to be what is fundamentally real, we take ourselves to be primarily or exclusively sensuous and appetitive beings, and vice versa. The life of sensuality is thus a failure to understand the true nature at once of reality and of ourselves. This is, for example, the central theme of Plato's *Phaedo*, as announced by the opening word: *autos*, "yourself" (57a1). In orienting its attention to sensible things rather than to intelligible reality, the soul fails to recognize itself as intellectual, possessing divine, intelligible reality within itself. Likewise, the prisoners in Plato's cave not only take shadows of puppets for true reality, but also take shadows of "themselves and one another" for their true selves (*Republic* 515a5). The ascent to knowledge of intelligible reality is simultaneously a discovery of the true self. Later in the treatise (Chapters 10–12), Plotinus explains that the higher levels of reality are also higher levels of the self; see Introduction, p. 16.

1, 3–17 *The principle of . . . ignorance of him*: The fundamental question that Plotinus is addressing in the opening lines of the treatise is this: Why do humans live lives of sensuality, greed, lust, fear, anger, and other passions, untrue to our own nature as rational beings capable of intellectual knowledge and union with divine reality? Here as in other early treatises (IV.7 [2]; IV.8 [6]) he explains this in terms of the human soul's isolating itself from the governance of the cosmos as a whole that it shares with soul in general by directing its attention to a single body within the cosmos, apart from and in opposition to other bodies: " . . . fleeing the whole and standing apart [*apostasa*; cf. in the present treatise *apostasin*, 1, 8] in its distinctness and not looking toward the intelligible, becoming a part, it is isolated and is weak and is busy and looks to a part, and, in separation from the whole, descending upon one thing and fleeing from all else, it comes to and turns to that one thing battered in every way by the whole" (IV.8.4, 13–18; cf. IV.7.13, 9–13). Confining its concern narrowly to a particular body, the soul "begins acting by sense because it is hindered from acting by intellect" (IV.8.4, 24–25). Such a soul allows itself to be affected by what happens to that body and is thus subject to passions: see IV.8.8, 16–22; I.8.15, 12–18. This is the "descended" condition in which all humans begin life (I.1.11, 1–2; V.9.1, 1–7), and many never rise beyond it.

The soul's "badness" (line 4), then, does not consist simply in its animating a body, but in its doing so in such a way that the soul belongs to the body rather than the body to the soul (IV.8.2, 47). For as Plotinus explains, "It is not bad in every way for the soul to provide the body with the power to flourish and to be, because not all providence for what is inferior takes away from that which is provident, its abiding in the best" (IV.8.2, 24–26). It is possible for the soul to animate the body contemplatively, without directing its attention to the body and without being affected by it. In III.8, personified Nature describes her mode of informing bodies in this way: "And my contemplating makes what is contemplated, as geometers, while contemplating, draw; but I do not draw, but as I contemplate, the lines of bodies come to be as though falling out" (III.8.4, 7–10). The image is that of a geometer gazing upward while drawing shapes in sand with a stick. This is the way in which the world-soul animates the cosmos and the souls of the stars animate the celestial bodies (IV.8.2, 31–42). And Plotinus insists that this is attainable for human souls as well (I.8.5, 29–33). This is what he means when he says that "our endeavor is not to be out of sin, but to be a god" (I.2.6, 2–3; cf. IV.7.10,

30–40), and this is the way of life to which he is calling us in the present treatise.

1, 3–5 *The principle of . . . belong to themselves*: Plotinus now proceeds to describe the attitude or orientation wherein the soul's badness fundamentally consists. *Archē* should thus be taken to mean "principle," not "beginning" in a chronological sense.

1, 4 *badness*: Not, as usually translated, "evil" or "wickedness." The word *kakon* refers to "badness" in a general sense, including "harm," "damage," or "poor quality," as well as moral vice. For instance (to borrow an example from LSJ, s.v. *kakos*), *kakos iatros* means "a bad doctor," not "an evil doctor." In the present context all of these senses, including but not limited to the moral sense, are in play. The English word "evil" has inappropriately narrow, intense, and even sinister connotations, doubtless due in part to its purely accidental association with the altogether unrelated word "devil" (and perhaps also "vile"). Plotinus is describing wherein the imperfection or deficiency of human souls consists. This deficiency leads to morally bad deeds, but cannot simply be identified with them. See IV.8.5, 16–18.

1, 4–5 *audacity and becoming . . . belong to themselves*: These four expressions describe the cognitive, ethical, and spiritual condition wherein the soul's badness consists.

1, 4 *audacity*: The term *tolma* has a long history in Gnostic and Pythagorean traditions, and its use by Plotinus has been extensively studied and debated (see Rist, 1965; Armstrong 1967, 242–245; Baladi 1970, 65–98; Torchia 1993; Majumdar 2007, 214–223). In Valentinian Gnosticism, it refers to the rebellious act of the spirit Sophia that leads to the making of the cosmos, so that the cosmos itself comes into existence as a result of sin. The Neopythagoreans use the term *tolma* to refer to the "indeterminate dyad" (on which see below, 5, 6–9, 13–17) as the ontological principle that allows for multiplicity.

Plotinus seems to use the term in his own ways, which are related to both of these but identical with neither. He altogether repudiates the Gnostic myth of the making of the cosmos by a fallen or rebellious spirit, expressly referring to *tolma* (II.9.11, 19–22). In some places, he uses *tolma* to characterize the inferiority or deficiency of any level of reality in relation to its superior. Thus he says that intellect "dared [*tolmēsas*] to stand away from the One" (VI.9.5, 29). Again, he describes the soul in a plant as "the most audacious and mindless [*tolmērotaton kai aphronestaton*]" (V.2.2, 6), evidently meaning "least intellectual," "furthest from intellect." In the present passage, Plotinus uses *tolma* with reference to the human soul's rebellious self-isolation (see Commentary 1, 3–17), as a result of which it operates by sense rather than intellect and becomes subject to passions. It is in this sense that *tolma* is the "principle of badness" for the soul.

1, 4 *becoming*: Although the term *genesis* can be translated simply as "birth" (as in Armstrong and Atkinson), such a reading does not accord well with what Plotinus is saying here. It is not birth in the body as such that constitutes badness for the soul, but rather its "downward" orientation to sensible things. What Plotinus evidently means is the involvement of the soul's attention with "becoming," that is, sensible things in temporal process. Hence MacKenna's gloss "entry into the sphere of process" or Harder's "Eingehen ins Werden" conveys the sense better. Likewise Igal and Fronterotta give respectively "generación" and "génération" rather than "nacimiento" and "naissance."

1, 4–5 *the first otherness . . . belong to themselves*: "The first otherness" must not be taken in an absolute sense, since in metaphysical terms the first otherness in the descent from the One is found at the level of intellect (see 4, 31–35, 37–40). It must rather refer, like *tolma*, to the soul's self-isolation, as does the phrase "willing to belong to themselves": cf. IV.8.4, 11 and III.7.11, 15.

1, 6 *Since they appeared to delight*: Some translators (e.g., Atkinson, Harder, Igal) take the phrase *epeidēper ephanēsan hēstheisai* to mean, "Once they had appeared in this world, they delighted . . ." But this is a rather dubious reading. First, souls do not, strictly speaking, "appear" at the sensible level at all: even the most vicious soul is not a sensible thing. More importantly, *epeidēper* can signify logical or causal rather than temporal sequence: Plotinus is continuing his description of what is wrong with our souls, not recounting a chronological narrative of their life-history. "Appeared to delight," then, perhaps implies that this pleasure in independence is apparent rather than real delight, a "shadow-pleasure" (cf. Plato, *Republic* 586b8) as distinct from the true delight of the soul in the contemplation of intelligible being, analogous to pleasure in a dream as distinct from pleasure in waking life. For a parallel see I.6.5, 30–31: " . . . living a life of what [the soul] experiences through the body, taking the shameful as pleasing . . ."

1, 5–7 *independence and indulged . . . moved by themselves*: This must be taken as another reference to the soul's self-isolation, its "willing to belong to itself." The soul takes a perverse and inauthentic pleasure in operating as an isolated individual rather than as a member of the universal whole.

1, 7–8 *running in the . . . very far away*: "The opposite direction" means "downward," away from their divine principle. The term *apostasis* can mean simply "lapse, declension" or even merely "departure," but also carries political connotations of "defection" or "rebellion" (see LSJ, s.v. *apostasia*). Cf. IV.8.4, 6–8, where Plotinus says of unfallen souls that "in heaven with the whole [soul] they co-govern with it, like those who, being with a king who rules all things, co-govern with him." The implication would be that a soul which isolates itself is comparable to a rebellious (*apostasa*, IV.8.4, 13) provincial governor, who, instead of administering his province as a part of the whole, sets himself up as the independent ruler of his own territory in opposition to the rest of the empire. The term may thus serve as a political metaphor for the soul's self-isolation or *tolma*.

1, 11–12 *No longer, then . . . of their race*: *genos* here means "race," signifying at once "kind" and "origin," not, as in Armstrong and Atkinson, "birth." Plotinus' point is that the soul fails to recognize what kind of reality it is and its divine origin. Cf. 1, 28, "race and worth," and 2, 44, where we are told that our soul is "of the same kind" (*hohhomoeidēs*) with the souls of the cosmos and of the celestial bodies. The soul "scorns," that is, fails to honor itself, in that it fails to recognize its own divine nature.

1, 12–15 *honoring other things . . . from in scorn*: Badness for the soul consists in exteriority: as a result of its self-isolation, its narrow concern for the body that it animates in isolation from the cosmos as a whole, the soul directs its attention to that body and to the sensible things that affect that body *ab extra*, rather than to itself and the higher principles, intellect and the One, that can be found within itself. Cf. IV.8.4, 20, "caring for exterior things [*ta exōthen*]." A fundamental difference between sense and intellect is that what is perceived by sense is received from without, whereas what is known by intellect is possessed within the knower; cf. IV.6.2, 19–22; V.5.1, 20, 27, 51–66. Operating at the level of sense, the soul takes sensible pleasure as its good and pain as its evil (V.9.1, 1–7). Thus it becomes subject to passions such as fear, lust, grief, and anger. This is what it means for souls to "honor," "admire," "delight in," and "be dependent on" "all things rather than themselves," which in the present context clearly means sensible things. Exteriority, sensuality, and being subject to passions thus coincide as descriptions of the soul's badness or "descended" condition.

1, 16–17 *Thus it comes . . . ignorance of him*: Here Plotinus answers the question of the opening sentence. What makes the soul oblivious and ignorant of itself and its divine father is its orienting its attention to outward, sensible things and locating its good in these, rather than to itself and the higher principles, intellect and the One, that can be found within it. This reiterates the theme of "obliviousness" with connotations of disregard or scorn, rather than mere involuntary "forgetting." See Commentary 1, 1–2.

1, 17–19 *For that which . . . making itself inferior*: Taking sensible things as its good, as what it needs, as what complete it, the soul thus regards itself as dependent on and lesser than them.

1, 19–22 *but making itself . . . power of god*: Viewing sensible, corruptible things as superior to itself, the soul comes to regard itself as mortal, as perishable, as belonging to the realm of generation and corruption, and indeed as more subject to death, more ephemeral, than these things. *Thnētotaton pantōn hōn timai* cannot mean, as most translators (Armstrong, Atkinson, Fronterotta, Igal, MacKenna) take it, "most mortal of the things it honors," since we have just been told that the soul does *not* honor itself. Harder rightly translates, " . . . sterblicher als alle die Dinge hält die es hochschätzt." For the comparative use of the superlative see Smyth, §1434.

The whole account of the soul's descended condition is a profoundly existential description of human life, of what we take as good and how we regard ourselves in relation to other things.

1, 22–25 *Hence two ways . . . one and first*: Again we see that the entire concern is the direction of the soul's attention: inward and upward to itself and the higher principles on which it depends, or outward and downward to sensible things.

1, 25–27 *One, which we . . . by the soul*: As Armstrong remarks *ad loc.*, it is not clear "where, if anywhere" Plotinus provides such a treatise *de contemptu mundi*. In II.9, he argues against the Gnostics that to despise the sensible cosmos is to blaspheme the divine principles on which it depends and of which it is an image: if the image is evil and ugly, its original must be more truly evil and ugly. See II.9.5, 27; II.9.6, 59–60; II.9.8, 6–20; II.9.17, 26–27. In Chapters 2 and 4 of the present treatise, the soul's return to self-knowledge and its ascent to intellect begin, not with the contemptibility, but with the beauty and grandeur of the sensible cosmos, *qua* animated by soul and reflective of intellect. If the cosmos were truly contemptible, it could not be the starting-point for this ascent. Plotinus regularly argues that badness lies not in sensible things as such but in the soul's orientation to sensible things (cf. Brunner 1973, 66). For a strong presentation of the contemptibility of this orientation, which might well serve to awaken the soul to the shamefulness of its condition, see, e.g., I.6.5, 24–50. A discourse of this kind may be what Plotinus has in mind here.

1, 30–35 *For that which . . . to find them*: The turn to interiority begins with the soul's reflecting on itself as that which is seeking or thinking; cf. I.1.13, 1–3; IV.3.1, 8–12. There must be at least a potential sameness between that which seeks to know and that which is to be known, or knowledge would not be possible: cf. Aristotle, *On the Soul* (*De anima*), 3.4.429a15–18. This is not merely an arbitrary application of the ancient principle "like is known by like," but rather a recognition that knowledge consists in a coinciding or sameness between knower and known, between thought and reality (Aristotle, *On the Soul* [*De anima*], 3.4.430a3–6; 3.5.430a19–21, 431a1–2). For as Plotinus argues at length elsewhere (V.3.5, 18–28; V.5.1, 50–58), to the extent that thought remains different from the reality that it seeks to know, to that extent we have falsehood, error, or deception, not knowledge. Hence, unless soul and the higher realities it seeks to know are *syggenē*, "akin" or "of the same kind," it cannot know them. Cf. Plato, *Phaedo* 79d3, 84b2; *Republic* 490b4, 611e2. If the soul were itself a body, it could not possess, and thus know, incorporeal principles. The ascent must therefore begin with the soul's recognition of itself, "that which is seeking," as an incorporeal reality superior to body.

Chapter 2

Plotinus now develops the second of the two kinds of discourse mentioned above (1, 27ff.). Soul gives order, motion, life, value, and existence to the cosmos as a whole and to all the living things in it. Since it makes the cosmos, the sun, and the stars to be gods, it is itself a higher god. Our soul is of the same kind as the souls of the cosmos and of the visible gods.

2, 1 *all soul*: As in Plato, *Phaedrus* 245c5 and 246b6, to which Plotinus is here alluding, *pasa psychē* can mean either "all soul" or "every soul." In the present passage we must say "all soul," because Plotinus is not making the absurd claim that each individual human soul made the sun and the entire cosmos, but is rather saying that our souls are of the same kind (*homoeidēs*, line 44) as the soul of the cosmos. Indeed, we might gloss *pasa psychē* as "soul in general" or "soul as a whole," for Plotinus argues elsewhere (IV.3.2–5; IV.9.2–5) that all souls are in a significant sense one as well as many (IV.9.2, 26). He explains that soul as such, considered simply as a level of thought and reality below intellect and above body, is not the soul *of* anything (e.g., IV.3.2, 8–10, 55–56). This is what is often referred to today as "hypostasis soul." Both the soul of the cosmos, and all individual souls, are "from" this (IV.3.4, 15; IV.3.5, 15–16; IV.9.4, 7–8) and are "parts" of this, not in any corporeal or quantitative sense (IV.3.2, 10–49), but in the sense that each one is a distinct "coming forth [*prophora*] and activity" (IV.3.2, 52) of soul-as-such, soul *qua* animating this or that body. Since the world-soul, no less than human souls, is not simply soul-as-such or hypostasis soul but is the soul *of* a certain body, the cosmos itself, Plotinus calls it a "sister" of human souls (IV.3.6, 13). Thus every soul (the world-soul and each human soul) is "all soul" or "soul as a whole" in a unique way, and as such is both distinct from and one with hypostasis soul: "Each remains one and all together are one" (IV.3.5, 14). Plotinus explains this by means of his favorite comparison to theorems within a science (IV.3.2, 53–56; IV.9.5, 22–26): each theorem contains by implication the entire science, so that each one is not an isolable piece but rather a distinct articulation of the whole, and thus each theorem, although distinct from every other theorem, is the whole science in its own way. Plotinus uses the same analogy to express how each distinct form is the whole of intellect in a distinct way (V.9.8, 3–7), and indeed concludes that the many "souls are from one, and they are from one in the same way as intellect, divided and not divided" (IV.3.5, 15–17). See further Commentary 4, 26–27.

The soul of the cosmos, and each human soul, is thus soul *qua* animating a certain body, a distinct "coming forth and activity" of soul-as-such. Hence each human soul is the same in kind as the soul of the cosmos, and needs to recognize the dignity and divinity that it shares with the latter.

2, 2–4 *those that the . . . made the sun:* The parts of the cosmos and the living things in each part are named in ascending order of the elements, from earth to water to air to fire. For Plotinus' understanding of the sun and the stars as "visible gods," that is, living beings animated by perfectly rational souls, see I.8.5, 31–35; II.9.5, 4–14; II.9.8, 29–39.

2, 5 *made it a cosmos*: *Ekosmēsen* does not mean merely "adorned" (Armstrong), implying superficial decoration; nor does it mean merely "ordered" or "organized" (Atkinson, Fronterotta, Igal), which leaves out the connotation of beauty. Harder's "formte" or MacKenna's "formed and ordered" is better, suggesting at once order and beauty. The full meaning is "made beautiful by ordering," that is, made the world to be a cosmos, an integrated, organic, beautiful whole, rather than a disorderly mess or what Plato calls an "uncombined collocation" (*Philebus* 64e1).

2, 5 *it moves it around in order*: From at least the time of Thales (see Aristotle, *On the Soul* [*De anima*] 1.2.405a19–21), soul was understood as the principle of motion for bodies. The fundamental distinction between a living, that is, an ensouled or animated thing, and a non-living, that is, a soulless or inanimate thing, is that the former can initiate motion from within itself, while the latter can be moved only by being affected from outside itself. In *Laws* X, Plato develops this into an argument that the cosmos as a whole is ensouled (*Laws* 891e5–899b9).

2, 6 *being a nature . . . and makes live*: A body simply *qua* body is not living and cannot move itself. Hence soul, as the principle of motion and life for bodies, must not itself be a body; cf. Aristotle, *On the Soul* (*De anima*) 2.1.412a17–20. Thus soul is a different kind of being from the bodies that it animates.

2, 7–9 *And it must . . . them with life*: Bodies depend on soul to live and thus to be *qua* living things. In the absence of soul, a body is lifeless, inert, and subject to decomposition. Hence soul, as what enables bodies to live, move, and persist, is "more honorable," that is, a higher or nobler kind of reality than bodies.

2, 9 *but soul itself . . . "depart from itself"*: A very brief argument, based on Plato, for the immortality of soul. For a living body to die is for soul to depart from it, and it can die because it is made to be living by something other than itself, viz. soul. Unlike a body, soul does not depend on something other than itself in order to live, and so cannot die. As the principle of life for bodies, soul is not itself subject to death. Cf. the more extended presentation of the same argument at IV.7.9, 6–13: "For [soul] is the principle of motion, providing motion to other things, but is itself moved from itself, giving life to the ensouled body, but itself possessing [life] by itself, which it never loses because it possesses it by itself. For surely not all things have life from without, or it will go to infinity; but there must be some nature which is primally living, which must be indestructible and immortal by necessity, because it is the principle of life for others as well." Cf. Plato's argument at *Phaedrus* 245c5–246a2, from which the words "depart from itself" (245e9) are quoted, and also the argument at *Phaedo* 105c9–107a1.

2, 11–12 *Let another soul . . . the great soul*: "Another soul" here is the human soul which is seeking to understand the nature of soul in general, and thus its own nature; "the great soul" is the world-soul, the animating principle of the cosmos as a whole.

2, 14–19 *Let not only . . . and illuminating it*: This passage is rendered confusing by an unmarked shift in the sense of "quiet" (*hēsychos*) that seems not to be sufficiently noted by most commentators. At first (line 14), this term refers in a positive sense to the contemplative stillness of a soul that is free from external distractions. This is the sense taken up by Augustine in his famous paraphrase of this passage in *Confessions* 9.10. In the next sentence (lines 14 and 16), it at first appears to have the same meaning. But we then find that the stillness of this "universe at rest" is not peace in any positive sense but rather the inertness of a corpse (line 26), the stillness not of contemplation but of lifelessness.

2, 17 *greater*: Reading, with HS$_2$, *ameinōn*, rather than, with the Addenda ad Textum in HS$_2$, vol. 3, *akēmōn*. *Ameinōn* is supported by the similar expression at IV.3.17, 3; cf. HS$_2$ *ad loc.*

2, 17–23 *And from everywhere . . . which lay still*: Here Plotinus asks us to imagine the inert, lifeless universe "before soul" (25). But this must not be taken literally, as if the universe first existed in an inert state and then was brought to life by the advent of soul. As Plotinus makes clear at lines 26–27, the universe would not exist at all without the informing presence of soul. As the giver of form, soul not only moves or enlivens but makes the cosmos. Cf. V.9.3, 26–30; II.9.3–4; and esp. IV.3.9, 14–18: "We must understand that the terms 'entry' and 'ensoulment' are used for the sake of explanation and clarity. For there was no 'then' when the universe was not animated, or when body existed in the absence of soul, or when matter was not ordered into the cosmos." Plotinus' point is not that the universe once existed without being animated. Rather, he is arguing that any body—whether the universe as a whole or a particular body within it—would be lifeless without the quickening activity of soul. Hence soul is what gives life, and thus value (*axia*, line 25), to the body. And therefore, soul is greater than body (cf. Plato, *Laws* 896b10–c2).

2, 24 *wise*: The soul of the cosmos is intelligent (cf. Plato, *Timaeus* 30b8, 36e4; *Laws* 897b7–899b9); otherwise, it would have no apprehension of the forms according to which it shapes and orders the cosmos: cf. V.9.3, 30–32; II.9.4, 7–11.

2, 25–27 *before soul it . . . as someone says*: Here Plotinus makes it clear that without the "illuminating," that is, the informing activity of soul, the cosmos would not merely be inert and lifeless, "a dead body," but would not exist at all. Soul does not merely order the elements into the living cosmos, but provides the forms by which the elements themselves are what they are (cf. V.9.3, 26–30). Without soul, then, there would not even be earth, water, air, and fire, but only formless matter. But formless matter, having no intelligibility whatsoever, is not anything at all, and so, as Plotinus here says, is "non-being" (*mē on*). Cf.

II.4.16, 3. Matter, for Plotinus, is no positive reality in its own right and cannot exist by itself. It "exists" only as a partial deficiency or privation of form, in a thing that has some form. Thus Plotinus argues that matter is "the same as privation" (II.4.16, 3–4) and that as such it is enabled to "be" at all only by form, as the "unlimited," which would be nothing by itself, is "preserved," or enabled to be, only by "limit" (II.4.16, 11–13). We may imagine it as comparable to a hole, which is nothing in itself but is enabled to be only by the surrounding solid in which there is a hole. Thus, without soul that provides form, the cosmos would not even be the lifeless and disordered elements, but would be nothing at all. This total absence of form or being, symbolized by "darkness," is "abhorrent" in that it offers no satisfaction to the need of thought for something, some form, some intelligible content, to apprehend. As such it is "the absolutely ugly" (I.6.2, 15–16) from which thought recoils in revulsion and distress (II.4.10, 31–35).

2, 30–32 *For to all . . . small is ensouled*: Cf. I.8.14, 36–37, where Plotinus quotes from Sophocles, *Oedipus at Colonus* 54: "'All the place is holy,' and nothing is without a share of soul," and Armstrong's note *ad loc.*: "If Plotinus fully remembered what he was quoting, and the passion of love for the 'holy place' of Colonus with which the whole play is charged, this must be taken as one of the strongest affirmations of the goodness of the material world in the

Enneads. Soul is a god and the material world is holy as being the place where it dwells." The present passage is a similar affirmation of the goodness and beauty of the cosmos, in virtue of its being ensouled.

2, 30–38 *For to all . . . unity and ubiquity*: Since the cosmos as a whole is a living thing, there is no part of it that is not ensouled (cf. I.8.14, 36–37, cited in Commentary 2, 30–32; IV.3.9, 37–38). But this does not mean that soul, like the cosmos, is divided into mutually extrinsic parts. Any body, *qua* spatially extended, has "parts outside of parts": the parts of a body are separated from one another by being in different spatial locations. Hence no body can be present as a whole in any one place: it must have a left side and a right side, a top and a bottom, an inside and an outside, etc., and these are spatially distinct from each other. If soul were divided into such mutually extrinsic parts, it would itself be a body (VI.4.3, 30–31). But as Plotinus explains at length in VI.4–5, incorporeal realities such as soul or intelligible being are not divided in this way. If soul were extended along with body, so that each part of the body—whether an individual body or the entire cosmos—were animated by a different part of soul, there would be nothing to account for the organic unity or wholeness of the spatially extended body, and what affects different parts of the body (e.g., the hand and the foot) would not be experienced by the same soul (VI.4.1, 25–27). This is one of Plotinus' principal arguments against the Stoic doctrine that the soul itself is a body (IV.7.2–8). Since soul is not so divided, it must rather be an incorporeal power, and as such one same soul is present as a whole at every point in the cosmos. This presents a difficulty only if we fail to transcend sense-based imagination and therefore picture the soul as a body (VI.4.13, 2–6). If we can learn to think (not imagine) soul as an incorporeal power, we can understand how one same power animates the entire cosmos. The whole and same soul is manifested differently in different places by being received according to the capacities of different bodies: "What is present must be understood to be present for the capacity of that which receives" (VI.4.11, 3–4; cf. VI.4.14, 13–14; VI.5.11, 28–31; IV.2.1, 64–77). This principle applies not only to soul as received in body but to intellect as received in soul and to the One as received in intellect; see Commentary 3, 13–17 and 21–23; 5,17–19; 6, 46–49; 7, 5–18. The well-known scholastic maxim, "Whatever is received is received according to the mode of the recipient," is derived via Proclus from this Plotinian insight.

2, 37–38 *like to the father who engendered it*: Each form is present to its instances, and intelligible being as a whole is present to the sensible cosmos as a whole, without being divided into mutually extrinsic parts. Thus soul is like its "father," intellect or intelligible being, in this respect.

2, 38–41 *And the universe . . . the other stars*: The cosmos as a whole is itself a god precisely in that it is a living thing animated by a perfectly rational soul; cf. Plato, *Timaeus* 92c6–9: " . . . this cosmos, a visible living thing containing visibles, image of the intelligible, a sensible god, greatest and best, most beautiful and most perfect . . . " The same is true of each of the celestial bodies; see Commentary 2, 2–4.

2, 41–44 *and we ourselves . . . senior to them*: *Eiper ti* must mean, not, as most translators take it, "if [we are gods] at all," but rather, as Atkinson and Igal understand it, "if anything [is a god] at all." For the construction see Atkinson (1983, 40–41). This accords with the line of argumentation that Plotinus is pursuing here: if any sensible thing—the sun, the stars, the cosmos, or ourselves—is a god, it is so in virtue of soul; therefore soul, as that by which sensible things are gods, is itself a superior god.

2, 44–45 *But our soul . . . taking it purified*: Here Plotinus calls us back to a consideration of ourselves: since soul in general is such as we have found it to be, a divine principle superior to the body that it animates, so our own soul is a being of this kind.

2, 45–47 *you will find . . . that is bodily*: In many places, Plotinus distinguishes between what pertains to the soul proper or by itself, without involving the body, and what pertains to it only in association with the body. The former category includes only the soul's reasoning or intellectual activities (see below, 3, 17–20 and 10, 13–17); the latter category includes sensation and all the soul's sensual appetites.

In this, Plotinus is following Plato, who distinguishes, most clearly in the *Phaedo*, between the soul's operating "itself by itself," that is, engaging in intellectual apprehension, and its operating "in association with the body," by way of sense, and thus being subject to distractions, disturbances, appetites, fears, etc. (*Phaedo* 65b9–66e2, 79c2–d7, 82d9–83e3). The present passage recalls especially Plato's image of the soul as the sea-god Glaukos (*Republic* 611b9–612a6), who is covered with shells and seaweed: the divinity within represents the rational part of the soul, which this image identifies with what the soul really is, while the encrustations, which do not really pertain to the soul itself, represent the non-rational appetites. Plotinus refers expressly to this image at I.1.12, 12–17. But Plotinus is also following Aristotle, who clearly and repeatedly distinguishes between, on the one hand, the intellect in us, which he characterizes as separable, impassible, and strictly incorporeal in that it is not the actuality of any bodily organ (see *On the Soul* [*De anima*] 1.4.408b25, 29; 2.1.413a6; 3.4.429a24–27; 3.5.430a18, 24), and, on the other hand, "the composite" (*Nicomachean Ethics* 10.7.1177b28), that is, the composite of the rest of the soul and the body.

Aristotle identifies the former as what is most truly the self and as the divine element in us (*Nicomachean Ethics* 9.8.1168b29–1169a2; 10.7.1177b28–1178a3). Likewise, Plotinus distinguishes between the human being proper, the "true man" (I.1.10, 7), that is, the higher, rational soul that operates independently of the body, and the composite of lower soul and body, which he calls "the beast" (I.1.10, 6) or "another man" (VI.4.14, 23). The "accretions," then, are all that does not pertain to soul as such, but only to soul in association with the body (cf. IV.7.10, 8–13). These are not really anything added, but are rather a diminution or dilution of the soul's true nature: "You became less by the addition" (VI.5.12, 20–21); cf. I.6.5, 50–58, where such passions are compared to the dross that is removed in the refining process, leaving only the pure gold. "Purification," then, is the removal of all that is lower, leaving only what is proper to soul *qua* soul, that is, its rationality. It is then that the soul is revealed in its true nature, as divine (I.6.6, 13–15; IV.7.10, 13–19), and this is what we, as rational beings, truly are.

2, 47–49 *For all things . . . water and air*: Regardless of what elements they are made of, all things would be worthless without soul. The reference to fire is somewhat obscure, and some, e.g. Atkinson, emend the text from *kaion* to *kalon*, so that it reads, "What would be its beauty?" But this seems unnecessary. Plotinus apparently means that the activity-of-burning, which is the "life" of fire, comes about in virtue of soul. Cf. VI.7.11, 40–45: "Matter is not able [to be fire] in such a way that [fire] could come from it—if then what makes [fire] according to rational principle must [do so] as shaping, what could it be but soul [which is] able to make fire? But this is life and rational principle. . . . Wherefore Plato says that in each of these [elements] there is soul, in no other way than as making this sensible fire." See also III.8.2, 25–30.

2, 49–51 *But if a . . . else, admire yourself*: Again the exhortation to interiority, to direct our attention and admiration to ourselves as thinking souls, rather than to what comes to us from outside by way of the senses.

Chapter 3

Soul derives from and is an image of intellect, which is still more divine than soul. Reasoning, the proper activity of soul, is soul's mode of possessing what is found in a higher way in and as intellect.

3, 1–3 *Since the soul . . . ascend toward him*: The term *pisteusas*, "believing" or "trusting," perhaps suggests that the preceding chapter is intended not as rigorous philosophical demonstration but as persuasive exhortation to recognize oneself, *qua* soul, as superior to body.

3, 3–4 *You do not . . . things in between*: As usual (see, e.g., II.9.1, 12–19; II.9.2, 1–2), Plotinus rejects any unnecessary multiplication of levels: only intellect lies "between" soul and the One.

3, 4–5 *Grasp, then, what . . . this divine thing*: Soul is divine relative to body, as enlivening it; intellect is "more divine," that is, divine relative not merely to body but to soul itself.

3, 5 *upper region that neighbors*: The unusual word *geitonēma* is taken from Plato, *Laws* 705a4. It means not "neighbor" but "neighboring region": Plotinus' metaphor here is that of a place, not a person.

3, 6–12 *For although soul . . . as something else*: Plotinus' point throughout this passage is that soul is a discursively extended "image" of intellect: that is to say, it possesses and thus consists of the same content as intellect, but in a lesser, more "unfolded" (*exeiligmenon*: V.8.6, 10) mode of presentation and apprehension. This is what he means just below, lines 21–22, where he says that "there is nothing between but their being different, one [soul] of course as subsequent and as the recipient": the difference between intellect and soul is a difference not of content, but only of level of presentation, like the difference between a thing and its reflection. It is in this sense that soul is the *logos* of intellect, that is, the "word" which is the outward, extended expression of thought. The terminological distinction between the *logos endiathetos*, the word as a thought in the mind, and the *logos prophorikos*, the word as a spoken utterance, is of Stoic origin; see SVF 2.135. But a similar distinction can be found in Aristotle, *On Interpretation* 1.16a3, and, most importantly, in Plato, *Sophist* 263e3–5. The latter passage is especially relevant because Plato here stresses the sameness between thought "inside the soul" and uttered speech, which Plotinus is here using as an analogy for the sameness of content between intellect and its expression, soul. Cf. his use of the same analogy at I.2.3, 27–30: "As the spoken word is an image of that in soul, so [the word] in soul is an imitation of that in another. As then [the word] in utterance is divided relative to that in soul, so [the word] in soul [is divided] relative to that which is prior to it, of which it is interpretive."

Plotinus' reference to the two activities and the analogy of fire make the same point. The activity that "remains in" intellect is intellection itself, the activity that intellect is (V.3.5, 32–48); the "activity that exists as something else" is the discursive expression of intellect, the activity which is proper to and constitutive of soul *qua* distinct from intellect.

3, 11 *there*: That is, in intellect. As often, Plotinus uses this spatial metaphor to refer to intellectual apprehension and its content, intelligible being.

3, 12–13 *Since it comes . . . consists in reasonings*: Plotinus' point here is that discursive reasoning is the analogous mode in which intellection occurs at the level of soul.

3, 13–17 *and its perfection . . . thinks and effects*: This should not be taken literally as a temporal sequence, as if soul were first made to be in a state of potentiality, and subsequently completed, perfected, or actualized by intellect.

Soul does not exist prior to being informed by intellect
any more than the universe exists prior to being informed
by soul (see above, Commentary 2, 17–23, 25–27). Rather,
its perfection is its actualization, which is its being made
to be. Plotinus' point is that soul is constituted as soul,
and so made to be, in receiving its content, what it thinks,
from intellect. The *logoi* that are the contents of soul, or
"what it thinks," are the discursively articulated expressions and apprehensions of the forms that are the contents
of intellect. It is in this sense that reason, the mode of
apprehension proper to soul, is actualized "by intellect's
being seen." Here again we see the principle of reception
according to the mode of the recipient; see Commentary 2,
30–38. Soul, in receiving or possessing intelligible content
in its own, discursive, way, thus "effects" or brings about
its own contents. In this respect the relation of soul to
intellect is analogous to the relation of intellect to the
One: see below, 6, 46–49; 7, 5–18.

Throughout Plotinus' discussion of soul as an image
(*eikōn*, line 7) and expression (*logos*, line 8) of intellect, he
is emphasizing that intellect and soul are not two different
things over against each other, but are the same contents
at higher and lower levels, intellectual and discursive, of
cognitive apprehension. Plotinus' doctrine here is taken
up in Proclus' theory of "self-constituted" terms (*authu-
postata*) (*Elements of Theology*, 40–51), which have the
same content as the higher levels from which they derive

but possess that content in their own, lesser mode, and thus constitute themselves insofar as they are distinct from their causes.

3, 17–20 *And only these . . . such a soul*: As we have seen (2, 45–47), only rational activity is proper to soul as such. All lesser activities, such as sensing and appetition, come to it *ab extra*, not through its being soul but through its association with the body, and thus are "affects" of it.

3, 21–23 *For there is . . . intellect as form*: This makes it very clear that the only difference between intellect and soul proper is the mode, intellectual or discursive, in which each one possesses the same content. This content subsists primarily in and as intellect, as purely intelligible form, and in a secondary way in soul, as discursively received or apprehended.

3, 23 *But even the . . . intellective and simple*: The reference of "the matter of intellect" is unclear. Does it mean soul, which Plotinus sometimes calls "matter" in relation to intellect in that it is receptive of form from intellect (II.5.3, 14; III.9.5, 3; V.9.4, 10–12)? Or does it mean the material aspect of intellect itself, what Plotinus elsewhere calls "the matter there" or "the matter in intelligibles" (III.8.11, 4), and discusses later in the present treatise under the name of "the indeterminate dyad" (5, 6–9 and 13–17), and at greater length in II.4.2–5? Most commentators (e.g.,

Atkinson 1983, 68–69; Brunner 1973, 73; Fronterotta *ad loc.*) adopt the former interpretation, doubtless because Plotinus has just referred to soul as receptive in relation to intellect as form. But in the present passage Plotinus is expounding the greatness of intellect itself, so that it would make more sense if he were saying that intellect's own matter is beautiful. Although soul stands in relation to intellect as matter to form, soul is not strictly speaking the matter *of* intellect itself, and Plotinus does not use this expression elsewhere. Hence it may be that he means rather "the matter in intelligibles," that is, intelligible being itself considered in its aspect of receptivity or potentiality relative to the One. In that case, this remark must be taken as a parenthetical aside, emphasizing the greatness of intellect by observing that even considered in its material aspect it is beautiful, that is, intelligible. The matter of sensibles is privation of form, and as such is non-being and the absolutely ugly (see above, Commentary 2, 25–27). But "the matter there [in the intelligible] is being, for that which is prior to it is beyond being" (II.4.16, 24–25; cf. II.4.5, 22), and, as such, it is beautiful.

Chapter 4

Intellect is the archetype of the sensible cosmos, having as its content all intelligible being, without temporal extension. Being and intellect thus constitute a unity-in-duality. The five "greatest genera" from Plato's Sophist, *being, difference, sameness, motion, and rest, are found throughout intellect.*

4, 1–12 *But one might . . . ever at rest*: Another way of recognizing the greatness of intellect is to understand it as the "archetype" or paradigm of the sensible cosmos, that is, the reality of which the sensible is an image. Any sensible thing exists at all just insofar as it displays some form, some intelligible content, which, just *qua* intelligible, is satisfying to the soul and thus is that thing's beauty (I.6.2, 7–29). Hence all the being, all the form, all the beauty of the sensible, all that is given to sense-perception, and thus everything in the sensible cosmos, is found at the level of intellect, and is "more true," that is, intelligible, at that level of presentation and apprehension. "All these things together [that is, all that is sensible] are from there, and are more beautifully there" (V.8.7, 17). See also VI.7.12, 1–16, where Plotinus argues that intellect, as the paradigm of "this all," contains all the parts of the cosmos—sky, earth, water, air—and all the living things in them. "Here" and "there," of course, are spatial metaphors: "here" means "given to sense," and "there" means "given to intellectual apprehension." Thus the intelligible and the sensible are not, as is too often said, "two worlds," any more than a man and his portrait, or his reflection, are two men (cf. VI.2.1, 21–25). Rather, they are the same content at higher and lower levels of apprehension. "These sensations are dim intellections, but the intellections there are clear sensations" (VI.7.7.30–31). Cf. Armstrong, "Introductory Note" to VI.7, p. 79: "In the end we are left with the very strong impression that for Plotinus there are not two worlds but one real world apprehended in different ways on different levels." See also Deck (1991, 110): "Plotinus does not have two worlds, but only one. His world of true being is not, except metaphorically, a world above the everyday world. It is the everyday world, not as experienced by sense, by opinion, or by discursive reasoning, but as known by intellect, the Nous, the Knower."

Consequently, the ascent to intellect is not a passage from one world, one set of objects, to another, but is rather an ascent of the self to a higher mode of apprehension of the same content. To ascend to intellect is to be intellect, to be intellectual apprehension (e.g., V.3.4, 10), and thus to apprehend intelligible being—that is, being or reality itself, of which the sensible is a "dim" presentation, diluted by spatio-temporal extension—within oneself, as the content of oneself (V.8.10, 32–41; VI.5.7, 1–8).

4, 1–5 *if one marvels . . . animals and plants*: This celebration of the greatness and beauty of the sensible cosmos recalls Plato's *Timaeus*, especially the concluding words, cited above in Commentary 2, 38–41.

4, 7 *its own awareness and life*: The life of intellect is the activity of intellectual apprehension (cf. Plato, *Sophist*, 248e6–249a4, and Plotinus, V.3.5, 31–37; III.7.3, 9–17; VI.7.15, 1; VI.7.17, 12–26), and intellect itself is this activity, having intelligible being as its content, or what it apprehends (V.9.5, 4–10; V.3.5, 32–48). Thus it is at once being, life, and intellect. In this respect Plotinus' intellect is comparable to Aristotle's unmoved mover, who is at once being or reality (*ousia*) as intelligible content (*Metaphysics* 12.7.1072a26, 1072b20–23), intellect or intellection (*Metaphysics* 12.7.1072b20–23; 12.9.1074b34–35), and life (*Metaphysics* 12.7.1072b27–31), that is, the paradigmatic activity of which all other life-activities are lesser versions (*On the Soul* [*De anima*] 2.4.415a27–b9).

4, 9–10 *what is truly . . . fullness and intellect*: The Hesiodic phrase *epi Kronou bion*, "life in the age of Cronus" is a literary trope for the golden age; cf. Virgil, *Eclogue* 4.6. But

Plotinus also punningly explains *Kronos* as *koros kai nous*, "fullness and intellect": intellect is fullness in that it has all intelligible being as its content. *Koros* also means "boy, youth," and thus refers to intellect as the "son" generated by the One; cf. III.8.11, 39. Plotinus takes the genealogy Uranus-Cronus-Zeus as a mythological expression of the sequence One-intellect-soul, so that in this respect as well Cronus may be taken to represent intellect.

4, 11–12 *ever at rest*: As Plotinus explains in III.7, "On Eternity and Time," "rest" taken by itself would imply merely remaining the same through time and would thus still involve temporal extension. In order to grasp the timelessness of intelligible being, "we must understand eternity not only in terms of rest but also in terms of unity; and again, as unextended, so that it may not be the same as time" (III.7.2, 31–33).

4, 12–16 *For why seek . . . but by having*: Intellect does not know intelligible reality sequentially, one being after another, but rather "always already" (*aei ēdē*, VI.2.8, 10) possesses, that is, apprehends, all being. Hence it has, so to speak, nowhere to go: it lacks nothing and there is no reality that it does not know. Thus it is "perfect" or complete and neither needs nor is able to "increase," to become more than it is.

4, 15–16 *having nothing in . . . does not think*: This phrase could instead be translated, "having nothing in it that does not think" (so Armstrong and Igal): that is, there is no part of intellect which is not actively thinking. But Plotinus' point throughout this passage is that intellect is in no way deficient and cannot "increase" because it eternally knows all reality. Hence the context suggests that the phrase means there is nothing in intellect that intellect does not apprehend. It thus leads logically to the next clause, indicating that intellect has no need to seek because it always already possesses, or apprehends, all being.

4, 16–25 *And its blessedness . . . are the same*: Since intellect always already knows or possesses all beings, it does not pass from one to another, as if "seeking" or "acquiring" something that it does not yet have. Hence the thinking that is intellect involves no sequentiality, but rather knows all being "at once" (*hama*, III.7.3, 18) and "together" (*homou*, III.7.3, 37), without the extendedness (*adiastatōs*, III.7.3, 15; cf. III.7.2, 32 and 34; III.7.3, 37) that is constitutive of time. Nothing is left behind, or no longer, and nothing is still to come, or not yet. Thus in intellect there is no "was," or past, and no "will be," or future, but all being together simply is (III.7.3, 34–35). This all-at-once apprehension of intelligible being is eternity (III.7.3, 36–38). Both in the present passage and in III.7, Plotinus is paraphrasing Plato,

Timaeus 37e4–38a1: "The 'was' and the 'will be' are forms of time which have come to be, which we unthinkingly apply, not correctly, to eternal reality. For we say that it was and will be, but according to the true account only the 'is' belongs to it . . . " This in turn is a paraphrase and elaboration of Parmenides' account of being: "It neither once was, nor will be, since now it is, all together, one, continuous" (DK B 8.5–6).

Time, then, is found not in intellect but only at the level of soul, which "temporalized itself" (III.7.11, 30) in apprehending sequentially or, as Plotinus says here, "one thing after another" (lines 19–20), "always moving to the next and the later and what is not the same" (III.7.11, 17–18), rather than all together at once. Time, therefore, "is the life of soul in transitive motion from one way of life to another" (III.7.11, 43–45). This life "imitates" (line 18) eternity in that the extended, "part-by-part whole" that constitutes time is an "image" of the "unextended" and "jointless whole" that constitutes eternity (III.7.11, 52–56).

4, 25 *as if content . . . they are so*: All things in intellect's eternity are "content" in that they lack nothing (cf. III.7.4, 15), as distinct from things in time, which if deprived of their future cease to exist, because they do not have all their existence at once (III.7.4, 19–22).

4, 26–27 *Each of them . . . and all being*: As Plotinus explains in many places, each form or being contains all the others, so that each one is the whole of intelligible reality in its own way; cf. V.8.4, 6–11, 22–24; V.9.8, 3–7. This is best understood, once again, in terms of the analogy of theorems in a body of knowledge: see Commentary 2, 1. In a deductive science like geometry, the many theorems are logically interrelated in such a way that it is not possible to falsify or omit one while leaving the others intact. They are really distinct in meaning, but each theorem both implies and is implied by all the others, so that each one contains, and thus is, the entire science in its own distinct way. Likewise, intelligible reality consists of many distinct forms, but each form is not a separable "piece" but rather a distinct articulation of intelligible reality as a whole. The point is exceptionally well expressed by Dodds (1963, 291): "A perfect system of knowledge would be a perfect type of organic unity: each part would involve, and be involved in the existence of every other part, yet without any blurring of the articulations which keep each part distinct and unique. In the content of a well-ordered human mind we may see an approximation to such a unity-in-distinction; and if we think of this content as grasped together in a single intuition instead of being surveyed piecemeal we may get some notion of what 'intellection' is, and of the mode of being of the Forms."

4, 27–28 *intellect, by thinking . . . thinking and existence*: As Plotinus argues at length elsewhere (V.9.5–8; V.5.1–2; V.3.5), intellect and being are ontologically simultaneous and indeed coincide or "exist together" (*synuparchei*, line 30), constituting a unity-in-duality. Intellect cannot know intelligible being as something else, extrinsic to, apart from, or over against itself. If it did, then intellect in itself, apart from being, would be potential, and would be actualized *ab extra* by being. But in that case, intellect in itself would not actually be intellectual, that is, would not be the apprehension of being. As actual apprehension, intellect must "possess" being as what it apprehends, as its own content, so that "it is itself the things that it thinks" (V.9.5, 1–8). Further, if being were extrinsic to intellect, then what intellect actually has as its content, or knows, would not be being itself, but only an image, effect, or impression of being—what in modern terms is called a representation. But if what intellect actually has is different from being itself, then its thinking, the thinking which it is, is not true (V.5.1, 51–58; V.3.5, 18–25). This is why any representationalist theory of knowledge inevitably leads to skepticism. Conversely, being itself would in that case be inaccessible to intellect, and so would not be intelligible. "We must not, then, seek the intelligibles outside [of intellect] . . . or by depriving it of truth produce ignorance and non-existence of the intelligibles and even do away with intellect itself" (V.5.2, 1–4). In order to be knowledge, intellect must coincide with being; in order to be what is known, being must coincide with intellect. Precisely as the apprehension of being, intellect possesses being as its content; precisely as intelligible, being is what is given (*doteon*, V.5.2, 9) to intellect as its content. Apart from one another, therefore, neither intellect nor intelligible being would exist. In this sense, as Plotinus here says, intellect and being constitute one another, or enable each other to be.

4, 29–30 *But the cause . . . of both simultaneously*: A proleptic allusion to the One as "cause" at once of intellect and of being. Since intellect and being can exist only together, the condition for their togetherness is what enables and in that sense "causes" them to be. It is not the case that the One is primarily and fundamentally the cause of being, and only secondarily the principle for cognition, or vice versa. Rather, the One is the cause of intellect and being "simultaneously," that is, in their togetherness, precisely as the condition of this togetherness. Cf. VI.7.16, 22–31: "For this reason he [that is, the Good or One] is said [by Plato] to be the cause not only of reality but of its being seen. Just as the sun, since it is cause for sensibles of being seen and of coming to be and in some way of sight, is therefore neither sight nor the things which have come to be, so the nature of the Good, since it is cause of reality and intellect, and is light, by analogy, to the things seen there and to the seer, is neither the beings nor intellect but cause of these, providing by its light both thinking and being thought to the beings and to intellect." Just as the enabling condition of intelligibility, the One is the cause at once of being, as that which is intelligible, and of thinking, as intellectual apprehension.

4, 30–31 *For they are . . . from each other*: For the reasons just given, intellect and being are ontologically simultaneous: there can be no order of priority and posteriority between them. Intellect, as the apprehension of being, cannot be prior to being (V.9.7, 14–17). This rules out any interpretation of Plotinus as a "subjective idealist," for whom intellect would be temporally or ontologically prior and would then produce being within itself. But neither can being be prior to intellect, since being just is what intellect has as its content. Hence, as Plotinus explains at V.9.8, 11–21, although we may "think being prior to intellect" (V.9.8, 11–12), this is merely because in our imperfect, discursive thinking they are "divided by us" (V.9.8, 20–21), whereas in truth they are "one nature" (V.9.8, 17).

4, 31–33 *but this one . . . which is thought*: An exceptionally compact account of the unity-in-duality of intellect and being. As we have just seen, being and intellect cannot be extrinsic to one another; they "exist together" (*synuparchei*, line 30), and in that sense are "one." But this togetherness cannot be sheer identity. "Intellect" refers to the *act* of thinking; "being" refers to the *content* of thinking, that-which-is-thought. The intentionality of cognition demands that intellect, as cognitive act, be the apprehension *of* something: "Every intellection is from something and is of something" (VI.7.40, 6). In that sense there is a distinction within this unity between intellect, as act-of-apprehension, and being, as what-is-apprehended. "That which thinks must be one and two. For if it is not one, that which thinks will be one thing and that which is thought another . . . But if, on the other hand, it is one and will not also be two, it will not have anything which it thinks, so that it will not be thinking. It must therefore be simple and not simple" (V.6.1, 7–9, 12–13). Consequently, "Its intellection about itself must be of something different, if it is to be able to think itself as anything at all" (VI.7.39, 12–13). Apprehension or knowledge is a single occurrence which, necessarily, can be analyzed into act and content, the apprehending and the apprehended, the knowing and the known, two inseparable moments of a single reality. The very idea of "being together" or "coinciding" implies duality as well as unity. This does not mean that intellect and being are two different parts of a greater whole: in that case, they would once again be extrinsic to each other and would not coincide (V.3.1, 1–12; V.3.5, 1–3). Rather, the whole is both intellect, *qua* act-of-thinking, and being, *qua* that which is thought; and the very term "both" implies at once duality and unity. This necessary duality in the unity of intellect and being is Plotinus' principal objection to the Peripatetic doctrine that the first principle is intellect: since intellect, having as its content being, is not absolutely simple, it is necessary to look still higher, for an ultimate principle of unity which is the ground at once of all reality and of all thought. See VI.7.37–41, and the whole of V.6.

4, 33–41 *For there could . . . distinction is difference*: A highly succinct but exceptionally clear and cogent deduction of the "Platonic categories," the five "greatest genera" from *Sophist* 254c3ff.: being, sameness, difference, motion, and rest. These are the "primary genera" (VI.2.8, 43) in that each of them pervades or is found throughout the whole of intelligible reality, so that each more specific form is a distinct kind of being, sameness, difference, motion, and rest. Cf. III.7.3, 7–11 and esp. the extended discussion at VI.2.7–8 and 15.

4, 33–34 *For there could . . . and also sameness*: As we have seen, thinking, or intellectual apprehension, necessarily implies both sameness and otherness between intellect as act and being as content.

4, 34–35 *Thus intellect becomes . . . being, difference, sameness*: Armstrong translates, "These then are primary, Intellect, Being, Otherness, Sameness," and most others

(Atkinson, Fronterotta, Harder, Igal, MacKenna) translate similarly. But it is extremely unlikely that Plotinus means to add intellect as a sixth genus, additional to the five enumerated by Plato. Rather, he is discussing the nature of intellect, the level of reality above soul, and saying that the first things intellect "becomes," that is, is found to involve, are: being (as intelligible content); difference (because of the necessary distinction between thinking and that-which-is-thought); and sameness (because of the necessary coinciding of these).

4, 35–37 *But we must . . . if it thinks*: The "motion" in question is not temporal change or process, but rather the timeless, unextended activity of intellectual apprehension. Aristotle coins the word *energeia* to refer to activities of this kind as distinct from "motions" (*kinēseis*), but Plotinus adheres to Plato's usage of *kinēsis* to refer to both. See Gerson (2005, 41n60, 217; 2006, 297–298). This is how Plotinus interprets Plato's attribution of "life" and "motion" to "that which completely is" at *Sophist* 248e6–249d4. Thus he explains at VI.7.13, 16 that intellect "must therefore move to all things, or rather have moved." The shift in tense indicates that this "motion" is not an extended sequence in which intellect grasps first one thing and then another, and only eventually all things. Rather, the motion is "intellection which is not acting toward what is future, but toward what is already, or rather already and always already [*aei ēdē*] and what is always present" (VI.2.8, 9–10), so that "it has wandering that abides" (VI.7.13, 33–34). This changeless activity is what Plato calls the "motion of intellect" (*Laws* 897d3) and represents by the stationary motion of a sphere rotating in place (*Laws* 898a3–b3).

4, 37 *and rest, so . . . be the same*: Since this activity of intellectual apprehension involves no change, in the sense of alteration over time, and that which it apprehends is eternally the same, intellect also in this sense involves rest.

4, 37–39 *And we must . . . will be silent*: A reiteration of the point that thinking requires distinction as well as sameness between act-of-thinking and that-which-is-thought.

4, 39–40 *And also the . . . to each other*: Difference within intellect consists not only in the distinction-in-unity between being and intellect, but also in the mutual differentiation among the forms, or intelligibles, that are its content. Such differentiation is a necessary condition for intelligibility. This is Plotinus' version of the well known Spinozan and Hegelian principle *omnis determinatio est negatio*, all determination is negation: any form, any being, any thought-content, is that one definite being, that idea, and so is intelligible, and is itself, only in virtue of its difference from other forms, other beings, other thought-contents. Without such differentiation, there can be neither thinking nor being. "Thus [intellect] understands itself by being a variegated eye or of variegated colors . . . so that which thinks must grasp one thing different from another, and that which is thought, in being thought, must be variegated" (V.3.10.30–32, 40–42). Intelligible being as a whole, therefore, necessarily consists of a multiplicity of mutually differentiated beings, which are intelligible, are themselves, and so are beings, in virtue of their differences from one another.

4, 40 *But we must . . . common to all*: Sameness is found in intellect in that being and intellect coincide and thus are the same as well as distinct, and in that all the forms have certain characteristics in common: e.g., each is one, each is intelligible, each is a being, etc.

4, 41 *and "the distinction is difference"*: While having these common characters, the forms are also distinct from one another, and this, again, is the difference among them. Thus "each of the things that are thought brings out along with itself this sameness and difference" (V.3.10, 28–29).

4, 41–43 *The multiplicity of . . . produces quality*: Since the contents of intellect are multiple, they necessarily comport "number and quantity"; and since they differ from one another not only in number but as to what they are (e.g., "motion" and "rest" are two different ideas), they comport quality.

4, 43 *and from these . . . come the others*: In VI.2.21, and especially at VI.7.8–10, Plotinus explains how intellect necessarily unfolds itself into all the more specific forms, e.g., "man" and "horse." A more generic form contains its specifications, each of which is the whole in a different way (VI.7.9, 29–38). Thus intellect as a whole includes all intellects, that is, all different intelligible contents (VI.7.8, 27–29; VI.2.21, 3–6). Likewise, being, sameness, difference, motion, and rest include all the different ways of being, being the same, being different, being in motion, and being at rest, and these are the "other" forms. See VI.2.21, 24–32. In this sense "the others" come from intellect as the five greatest genera.

Chapter 5

Since intellect is multiple, it cannot be the first principle. As a determinate multiplicity or number, it depends on the One, and can be analyzed into the indeterminate dyad, as that which underlies determination, and the determination that it receives from the One.

5, 1 *This god beyond . . . then, is multiple*: Intellect is a higher level of divinity than soul (cf. 3, 6). The preceding chapter has demonstrated the multiplicity of intellect, in preparation for showing that we must ascend still higher to find the absolute first principle.

5, 1–2 *and it is . . . will to desert*: *Hyparchei* here must mean "is possible" (as in Atkinson; for this construction with dative and infinitive see LSJ, s.v. *hyparchō*) rather than "exists" (as in Armstrong and MacKenna): soul must actively turn toward the contents of intellect in order to be so conjoined with them.

5, 3 *Having drawn near . . . [the soul] asks*: Reading, with the MSS, *zētei*, "asks," rather than, with HS₂ and Armstrong, the proposed emendation *zēi aei*, "lives forever." Plotinus argues that all soul is immortal by nature, so its immortality is not conditional upon its adherence to intellect (see above, 2, 9 and Commentary, and especially IV.7.12–14). Reading *zēi aei* also entails an irrelevant reference to the soul's immortality followed by a sudden unheralded leap to the question of intellect's origin. *Zētei*, "asks," "seeks," "inquires," on the other hand, leads smoothly into the question that follows. See Atkinson (1983, 105–106).

5, 3–4 *Who is it . . . that generated this?*: Plotinus' use of personal (masculine) as well as impersonal (neuter) terms with reference to the One is noteworthy, and accords with the mythological treatment in this work of soul, intellect, and the One as an ascending series of deities.

5, 4–5 *The simple, he . . . its being many*: Multiplicity depends on unity, for there can be no multiplicity unless each member of it is *one* and all the members taken together constitute *one* complex whole. Since, then, unity is a precondition for multiplicity, no multiplicity can be the absolute first principle. Having shown in the previous chapter that intellect is multiple, therefore, we can now infer that it is posterior to "the simple," that is, that which is not in any way multiple. Intellect and being, as a unity-in-duality and as a multiplicity of intelligible forms, depend on "the simple" in order to exist, and in this sense "the simple," that is, the One, is the "cause" (4, 29) of intellect and being. Cf. V.3.16, 10–16: "That which is prior to [intellect and the intelligible cosmos] and generated it is neither intellect nor an intelligible cosmos, but simpler than intellect and simpler than an intelligible cosmos. For many does not come from many, but this many comes from the not-many; for if this too were many, not this but something else prior to this would be the principle. It must then be really concentrated [*systenai*] into one, outside all multiplicity and any simplicity whatsoever, if it is really simple." The phrase "outside . . . any simplicity whatsoever" makes it clear that the One is not simple in any positive sense; if it were, it would have simplicity as an attribute and so would be not simple but complex, because there would be a distinction within it between the attribute and that which has the attribute. The term "simple" (*haplous*, line 4) as applied to the One, like the name "One" itself, is purely negative in meaning, signifying only "not complex or many." Cf. V.5.6, 26, 30–33: "Perhaps even this name, 'One,' means denial in relation to the many . . . For perhaps this was said, so that he who seeks, beginning from this, which signifies complete simplicity, may in the end negate even this . . . "

5, 5–6 *he who makes . . . is not first*: In ancient mathematical thought, one is not a number but the principle of number. This point, on which the whole of Chapter 5 depends, is exceptionally well explained by Klein (1968, 46–49): "The fundamental phenomenon which we should never lose sight of in determining the meaning of *arithmos* [that is, number] . . . is counting, or more exactly, the *counting-off*, of some number of things. . . . Only that can be 'counted' which is *not one*, which is before us in a certain number. . . . The 'unit' as such is no *arithmos*. . . . The smallest number of things or units is: *two* things or units. . . . The unit . . . has the character of a 'beginning' or 'source' (*archē*) such as makes something of the nature of 'counting' originally possible." Any actual number, therefore, is a finite multiplicity of units (Klein 1968, 51). As such, "number is not first," but depends on the unit, which can therefore be said to "make" number. See Aristotle, *Metaphysics* 10.1.1052b24: "The unit is the principle of number *qua* number."

5, 6 *unity*: Throughout this chapter, *to hen* means both "unity" which is the principle of number, and "the One," the first principle of reality itself, with no clear distinction in Plotinus' thought between these meanings. The decision to translate it in some places as "unity" and in others as "the One" is therefore somewhat artificial. But to translate it throughout as "the One" (as do Armstrong, Atkinson, Harder, and Igal, but not MacKenna and Fronterotta) is to risk losing sight of the specifically arithmological nature of Plotinus' argumentation. This twofold meaning may be explained by Plotinus' thought operating simultaneously on two planes, the arithmological and the metaphysical. On the arithmological plane, *to hen* signifies unity as the principle of number; on the metaphysical plane, *to hen* signifies the One as the principle of intelligible being. But these planes coincide, because the "number" in question here *is* intelligible being itself, as Plotinus expressly says at line 9: "Number in the sense of reality [*ousia*]." The unity which is the principle of number in this sense is the One itself.

5, 6–9 *For in fact . . . sense of reality*: The whole of Chapter 5 depends on understanding intellect or intelligible being, *qua* multiple, as number, and hence as a composite of limit or determination and a "substratum" (line 14), in itself unlimited, that has or underlies this determination. "Number" (*arithmos*) signifies "determinate multiplicity" (see Commentary 5, 5–6). Since intelligible being has been found to be such a multiplicity, it can therefore be called "number" (4, 41). Thus Plotinus explains (line 9) that the "number" at issue here is intelligible reality (*ousia*) itself. As a determinate multiplicity or number, intelligible reality is neither absolutely one nor altogether unlimited. Cf. VI.6.1, 1–2: "Is, then, multiplicity a falling away from unity [or the One], and unlimitedness a complete falling away by being numberless [*anarithmon*] multiplicity?" In that intellect is a limited multiplicity or number, it may be analyzed into that which has or possesses limit, and the limit that it has. The former, considered in abstraction from limit, is in itself unlimited (see VI.6.3, 12–15). This is what Plotinus here calls "the dyad" (line 6), which is "indeterminate in itself" (line 8). It is the "substratum" (line 14) in that it is that which underlies determination or limit. Since limit is an imposition of unity on that which, in itself, lacks unity, limit derives from unity itself, or the One. Thus the indeterminate dyad "has" unity, or the One, "as what determines it" (lines 7–8). Intellect, therefore, as a determinate multiplicity or number, may be said to "come from" (line 15) the indeterminate dyad and unity or the One.

According to Aristotle (*Metaphysics* 1.6.987b19–27), Plato himself, under Pythagorean influence, held just such a position, reducing all determinate multiplicity, including that of the forms themselves, to two principles: the One and the unlimited dyad, also known as "the great-and-small" (see Dillon 2003, 40–42; Nikulin 2012, 17–18). This theory may be adumbrated in the *Philebus*, where determinate multiplicity, or number, is found to lie "between the unlimited and the one" (16c9–e2) and being is understood to consist of limit, the unlimited, and the "mixture" of these (23c9–d1). Such a doctrine, in a variety of versions, was held by Speusippus (Dillon 2003, 40–48) and other middle Platonists and Neopythagoreans (see Sextus Empiricus, *Against the Professors* [*Adversus Mathematicos*] 10.261–262), and would have been regarded by Plotinus as authentic Platonic teaching. "The unlimited" is what Plotinus here calls "the indeterminate dyad" (lines 6–8, 14) and elsewhere "the matter there" (e.g., II.4.3, 13; II.4.4, 9; II.4.16, 24–25; II.5.3, 10), "divine" matter (II.4.5, 15), or "the matter in intelligibles" (III.8.11, 4). Considered by itself, in abstraction from the determination that it possesses, this is purely indeterminate, receptive, or potential: "For if you take away [from being] in your mind the variety and the shapes and formative principles and thoughts, what is prior to these is shapeless and indeterminate and none of the things that are on it and in it" (II.4.4, 18–20).

This theory, however, must not be taken to mean that, according to Plotinus, the indeterminate dyad actually exists prior to receiving determination and thus independently of the One. Sextus Empiricus, *Against the Professors* (*Adversus Mathematicos*) 10.282, reports that the theory of the One and the indeterminate dyad took two forms: a dualist form, according to which the One and the indeterminate dyad are two equiprimordial and mutually irreducible principles, and a monist form, according to which the dyad itself derives from the One, which is thus the sole truly first principle (see Torchia 1993, 14–15). Plotinus, of course, adopts the latter position. For the purely unlimited or indeterminate cannot exist by itself: devoid of any unity whatsoever, it would be not multiplicity but absolutely nothing (VI.9.1, 1–3). The dyad or substratum therefore depends, in order to exist, on the limit that it receives from the One. As Plotinus argues elsewhere, limit "preserves [the unlimited] in existence" (II.4.16, 12; see the discussion of the matter of sensibles in Commentary 2, 25–27). Hence the indeterminate dyad, or the unlimited, cannot be a principle in its own right, independent of the One. What is generated from the One is intellect or intelligible being itself (see, e.g., V.5.6, 1–4, 10). Within this, as a determinate multiplicity or number, we can distinguish the aspect of determination and the aspect of that which is determined. The latter is the dyad, the substratum, or "the matter in intelligibles." This has no existence of its own, independent of or apart from the determination that it possesses: "For the substratum there [that is, in the intelligible] is reality [*ousia*], or rather, considered with what is on it [that is, determination] and [as a] whole, it is illuminated reality" (II.4.5, 22–23). Since it exists only as a component or aspect of intelligible being, the dyad itself must be reduced, or traced back, to the One. In the present passage, therefore, where Plotinus is presenting being, *qua* determinate multiplicity or number, as a composite of determination and an indeterminate substratum, he emphasizes that this substratum itself, the indeterminate dyad, is "second" or posterior to and "comes into being from" unity or the One (line 7).

5, 9 *reality*: *Ousia* here, as throughout the Platonic tradition, means "reality-as-intelligible-form." The traditional translation of *ousia* as "substance" is hopelessly misleading, since "substance" in modern English does not carry the connotation of intelligibility, and indeed tends to suggest its very opposite, materiality. Reality in this sense, *qua* determinate multiplicity, is number.

5, 9 *soul is a number*: Xenocrates famously defined soul as a "self-moving number" (Heinze 1965, fr. 60) drawing on Pythagorean theory and perhaps on Plato, *Timaeus* 36e6–7. See Dillon (2003, 121–122). At VI.6.16, 44–45, Plotinus, referring to this passage in Plato, says that according to Plato, soul "is neither body nor any magnitude; the soul is therefore a number, if it is a reality [*ousia*]." In other words, soul is a number in the sense that it is not a body but rather an incorporeal formative principle or *logos*. Cf. Atkinson (1983, 114): "P[lotinus] wants us to take number and substance [that is, *ousia*] almost as synonyms. Anything which is a substance is a number." In the following lines of the present treatise, Plotinus explains that such principles are what determine and thus generate bodies, which are therefore ontologically posterior to number in the sense of formative principle.

5, 10–11 *For masses and . . . beings, are posterior*: "Thick," here, means spatially extended, so that "masses" or "thick things" means simply bodies. These, although taken for reality, or beings, at the level of sense-perception, in fact depend, in order to have size, shape, and magnitude, and so in order to be bodies, on number, which in itself is not sensible but intelligible. Hence bodies are posterior to intelligible number. "So form comes to [matter] bringing all things to it; the form possesses everything, both magnitude and whatever is with rational principle [*logou*] and by this" (II.4.8, 23–25).

5, 11–13 *And again, in . . . and rational principle*: The concept of "spermatic *logoi*" as principles that determine the growth and development of living things is of Stoic origin (see SVF 2, 1027; 2, 1132). But for the Stoics these *logoi* are themselves corporeal. In opposition to this, Plotinus observes that the power of seeds to develop into complete living things is rather "what is not seen," that is, the *logos* which is an intelligible formative principle in them. In this he follows Aristotle's argument that nature, understood as an intrinsic principle of motion and development in natural things, is more fundamentally form than matter: see *Physics* 2.1.198a30–b18. So, for Plotinus, nature, as the actualizing and moving principle in sensible things, is *logos* in the sense of "rational formative principle"; cf. III.8.2, 20–30, and VI.7.11, 17–28. In the present passage he interprets these intelligible formative principles as numbers.

5, 13–14 *So what is . . . principle and intellect*: As we have seen, the dyad would be nothing by itself, but "considered with what is on it [that is, determination] and [as a] whole, is illuminated reality" (II.4.5, 22–23), that is, intelligible being, the forms, and intellect.

5, 14–17 *The dyad, understood . . . be in it*: As a determinate multiplicity or number, intelligible being can be reduced to, and in that sense comes from, the indeterminate dyad, as that which receives or possesses limit, and unity, as that which provides limit. Each member of this determinate multiplicity is a form, that is, a distinct composite of the indeterminate and limit. Intellect is "shaped," that is, determined as to what it is, by the forms that are its content.

5, 17 *It is shaped . . . another by itself*: Plotinus develops this point more fully at 7, 5–18, especially 10–15, where he explains that in one sense the One generates intelligible reality or the forms, and in another sense intellect generates the forms as its own content. Intellect is "shaped" by the One in that each form, or being, is determinate (7, 23–26; cf. V.5.6, 5–6), and all determination derives from unity. Hence the One is the ultimate principle of determination and is thus the "cause" (5, 5) of being as a determinate multiplicity or number. But intellect is "shaped by itself" in that it is intellect's pluralizing mode of possession that articulates what it receives into a multiplicity of distinct intelligible beings. Thus intellect generates its own content, as the multiplicity of determinate forms, by its mode of receptivity. Here again we see the principle of reception according to the capacity of the recipient (see Commentary 2, 30–38 and 3, 13–17), and hence the "self-constitution" of the lower level in its distinction from its superior (see Commentary 3, 13–17).

Plotinus often presents this twofold "shaping" of intellect in terms of two moments or phases in the generation of intellect from the One (V.2.1, 7–13; V.3.11, 4–16; VI.7.16, 13–22). In the first moment, intellect proceeds from the One in an inchoate or indeterminate state. In the second moment, this "turns back" to the One and receives determination from it, thus becoming actualized as intellect proper, having as its content the multiplicity of intelligible beings. On the two-phase generation of intellect see Rist (1962) and Igal (1971). These two moments correspond respectively to the indeterminate dyad or "the matter in intelligibles," and the determination in virtue of which it becomes intelligible being (II.4.5, 15–17, 32–33). But these phases must not be understood sequentially, as if intelligible matter or the dyad actually existed in a pre-intellectual or indeterminate state. As purely indeterminate and potential, this would not actually be anything at all. What comes from the One, in the sense of depending on it, is not the indeterminate dyad *qua* indeterminate, or "divine matter" without determination, but rather intellect or being itself. Within this, as determinate, we can discern the aspect of that which possesses and in that sense "underlies" determination, and the aspect of determination that it has. The first, considered by itself, may variously be called "the indeterminate dyad," "the matter in intelligibles," "sight not yet seeing," "unformed sight," etc. See V.3.11, 5 and 12; V.4.2, 7. The story of the two moments or phases is simply a way of describing being or intellect as receptive of determination from, and thus dependent on, the One.

This can also be expressed by saying that intellect, as a multiplicity of determinate forms, and therefore as dependent (5, 4–6), is actualized by the One, and thus involves an aspect of potentiality (III.8.11, 2). This potentiality is represented by the indeterminate dyad, which is actualized or informed by receiving determination from the One. Thus intellect is "shaped" by the One, as source of determination, and is "shaped" by itself, as receptive of determination.

5, 18 *like vision in act*: Cf. III.8.11, 1–6. Considered apart from that which is seen, vision is only a potentiality; cf. Aristotle, *On the Soul* (*De anima*) 2.5.417a7–8. There can be no actual vision, or seeing, without something seen. Thus vision is actualized by the seen as what provides its content, determining it as a seeing *of* this or that, and thus letting it be actual seeing or "vision in act." In this sense it is "shaped" by the seen. But in another sense it is "shaped" by itself, as taking in or receiving the seen according to its own mode of receptivity. Thus "vision in act," in relation to that which is seen, is analogous to intellect in relation to the One, as an actualized potentiality, determined in one way by the One and in another way by itself *qua* receptive.

5, 19 *for intellect is sight which sees*: Intellect proper is actualized apprehension, having as its content the One *qua* received and thus not the One itself (*autoen*, V.3.12, 51; see below, Commentary 7, 20 and 11, 7–10) but rather the multiplicity of intelligible forms, constituted as multiple and determinate by intellect's mode of receptivity or possession.

5, 19 *and both are one*: As actualized sight is one with, or just is, the act-of-seeing, having as its content that which is seen, so actualized intellect (*nous*) is one with, or just is, the act-of-thinking (*noēsis*), having as its content that which is thought, intelligible being.

The upshot of Chapter 5 as a whole is that intellect, as a determinate multiplicity or number, is posterior to the One. This posteriority can be variously represented as indeterminacy, receptivity, or potentiality, which is determined, informed, or actualized by the One. Thus this chapter passes naturally into the next.

Chapter 6

How does intellect, as multiple, come from the One? It must do so without any motion on the One's part. The metaphor of emanation helps us conceive such production. Intellect is an expression of the One just as soul is of intellect.

6, **1** *whom*: Note once again the personal (masculine) form with reference to the One.

6, **1–8** *And how did . . . back to that*: As at V.9.14, 2–5, the question is, "How does being come from the One?" not "Why does the One generate being?" To ask, "Why does the One generate?" would be to misunderstand what it means to say that the One generates being. This means only that all things depend on the One as the enabling condition for their existence; it does not mean that the One performs an activity of generating. "Even to say 'cause' is not to predicate some accident of it, but of us, in that we have something from it, while that is in itself; but speaking precisely, one must not say 'that' or 'is' . . . " (VI.9.3, 49–52). The One itself, not any act or motion distinct from the One itself, is the "why" of beings: VI.8.11, 8–9; VI.8.14, 31–32. See further Commentary 6, 28–39.

6, 6 *that*: Here Plotinus switches from the masculine to the neuter form. Plotinus uses the phrase "the One" (*to hen*) much less frequently than most translations suggest. Far more often he uses only the demonstrative pronoun *ekeinos/ekeino*, no doubt in order to be as indefinite as possible and to avoid suggesting that the first principle is one in any positive, numerical, or quantitative sense. Cf. V.5.6, 26–34; V.4.1, 8–9. The present translation adheres to Plotinus' usage as closely as possible by translating *ekeino* (neuter) as "that" and *ekeinos* (masculine) as "he," and using "the One" only where Plotinus actually uses the phrase *to hen*.

6, 8–12 *In this way . . . way to pray*: Armstrong *ad loc.* calls this "the only explicit reference to genuine prayer in Plotinus." But cf. the close parallel at IV.9.4, 6–7, as well as V.8.9, 13–18 (although in that case the invocation is directed to intellect, not to the One), and V.5.3,12–13, where the One is compared to the Great King at whose appearance "they pray and make prostrations."

6, 11–12 *alone to the alone*: This phrase occurs elsewhere in the *Enneads*, most famously as the concluding words of VI.9 (VI.9.11, 51); see also I.6.7, 9. But it is often misunderstood.

Plotinus is not referring to a self-isolation, which both at the opening of the present treatise and elsewhere (IV.7.13, 11–13; IV.8.4, 13–18) he associates with the fall of the soul into sensuality and passions (see Commentary 1, 3–17). Cf. Brunner (1973, 81): "The fact that [the word 'alone'] is presented in the plural: *monous pros monon*, is perhaps not without significance: Plotinus does not enclose himself in a solitary experience as sometimes said. 'To go alone to the alone' means for him to go there as the soul alone, without the accompaniment of the corporeal passions and denuded of that which is alien to God . . . " The term "alone" refers to the soul's purification from passions and the lower self. The purified soul is "alone" in that it is purely itself, free from association with the "other man" (VI.4.14, 23), that is, the composite of lower soul and body, the lesser self which is subject to passions (I.2.6, 3–10). In the present passage, therefore, the reference to the soul's being "alone" should remind us of the earlier statement at 2, 44–45 that "when you look at [our soul] without accretions, taking it purified, you will find the same honorable thing that we said soul was."

6, 12–15 *Since, then, he . . . that appeared first*: More than once Plotinus compares the One to the god who dwells within a temple, and intelligible being to the statues that stand outside; cf. VI.9.11, 17–22. Intellect or being is "the statue that appeared first" in that it is the first or highest level of manifestation from the One. Being "appears" in that it is given to intellect. As statues are images of the god, but are not the god himself, so the forms, or beings, are images of the One: every being, in that it is a being, is a manifestation of the principle of being, but is not that principle itself.

6, 13 *beyond all things*: Cf. Plato, *Republic* 509b9. The One is beyond all things in that, as the principle by which all things exist, he is neither one of all things, nor all things taken together as a totality. "All things" (*hapantōn*) here includes and indeed refers primarily to the intelligibles or forms, not merely to sensible things. Cf. V.5.6, 9–13, and below, 7, 19.

6, 15 *appearing in this way*: Again the question is how we are to understand the derivation of intellect from the One; cf. above, 6, 1–2.

6, 15–27 *For everything that . . . way at all*: The passage as a whole is an argument to show that the generation of intellect must not be understood to involve any motion or activity on the part of the One.

6, 15–16 *For everything that . . . which it moves*: Motion, here, refers not merely to locomotion or other temporally extended processes, but, analogously, to any activity, including non-temporal activities such as the "motion" of intellect; see Commentary 4, 35–37. Any motion, in this sense, has an end (*telos*) in the sense of a perfection or fulfillment. See Aristotle, *Metaphysics* 9.8.1050a7–9: "Everything that comes to be proceeds toward a principle [*archēn*] which is also an end [*telos*]; for the principle is that for the sake of which, and becoming is for the sake of the end." Cf. Plotinus, III.8.7, 17: "For all things their principle is their end [*telos hapasin hē archē*]." The "end," in the sense of fulfillment, is the "beginning" in the sense that it is the principle that accounts for the motion or activity. Thus the activity of intellection has an end, the knowledge or possession of being, although this end is not the result of an extended process but is always already achieved (see Commentary 4, 35–37). It is in just this sense of being perfected that intellect, as "seeing sight," involves potentiality, although it never exists in a non-actualized condition. See Commentary 5, 17 and 18.

6, **16–17** *Since there . . . that it moves*: As the first principle, the One cannot have an end or perfection. If it did, that end (*telos*) would be its principle (*archē*), and therefore the One would not be the absolute first principle. Hence we cannot attribute motion or activity in any sense to the One.

6, **17–19** *but if something . . . turned toward itself*: Since no motion can be attributed to the One, it follows that the generation of intellect must not involve any motion on the One's part.

The final clause of this sentence is disputed. It may be translated as here, " . . . while that [that is, the One] is always turned toward itself," or " . . . while it [that is, the product] is always turned toward it [that is, the One]." Since Plotinus does not strictly observe the distinction between *heauto/hauto* (reflexive) and *auto* (demonstrative), and the pronoun in line 18 may be read in either of these ways, both interpretations are possible. The former reading is favored by Armstrong, Hadot (1963, 94), Harder, Igal, MacKenna, and Rist (1967, 268n44); the latter by Atkinson (1983, 135–140), Brunner (1973, 82), and Fronterotta.

The principal reasons given in support of the latter reading are these: To say that the One is "turned toward itself" would be to ascribe a motion to the One, whereas this is what Plotinus is ruling out here; and, on the other hand, Plotinus routinely describes the generation of intellect in terms of intellect's "turning back" to the One, as he does in the present treatise at 5, 17–19 and 7, 5–18. See Commentary 5, 17. But this reading seems forced and does not suit the context. First, as we have seen, Plotinus very frequently uses *ekeinos/ekeino* to refer to the One. In the present chapter he does this so many times (2, 6, 8, 10, 12, 17, 24, 28, 42 [twice], 46, 48) that it must be regarded as virtually a technical term. It would be very strange, therefore, if here and here alone in this chapter *ekeinou* referred instead to intellect. Second, what is at issue in this passage is the motionlessness of the One, its having nothing "toward which" it could move. The "turning back" of intellect to the One does not follow logically from this, whereas the One's being "turned to itself" may be taken to mean only that the One, unlike everything that moves or acts, is not oriented toward an end beyond itself. See Igal (1971, 135).

Understood in this way, the expression is paralleled by various formulations in VI.8. Here Plotinus denies that the One "has any activity toward another [*eis allo energe-ian*]," and says that the One is "not related to anything [*pros ouden*]" (VI.8.8, 11–13). Then, after warning us that he is speaking improperly for the sake of persuasion (VI.8.13, 4–5), he attributes self-directed activity to the One, and subsequently characterizes the One as "love of himself" (VI.8.15, 1). In a context very similar to that of the present passage, Plotinus then remarks that whereas all things "look to" the One, he, on the other hand, does not look to them but is rather "borne to his own interior" (VI.8.16, 12–13; cf. 19–21). Finally, Plotinus says that the One is "related to himself and toward himself [*pros auton kai eis hauton*], so that he may not be related to an exterior or to an other, but altogether to himself" (VI.8.17, 25–27).

Thus it is by no means unparalleled for Plotinus to describe the One's superiority to all relation by saying that he is "turned toward himself." Like all these "improper" expressions, then, the One's being "turned toward itself" in the present passage may be taken to mean merely that the One is not related to or oriented toward anything beyond itself, because if it were so related it would not be the absolute first principle. The point of the present sentence, then, is that intellect is generated from the One without the One in any way moving or being related to intellect.

6, **19–22** *(Generation in time . . . cause and order)*: The text at this point is disputed and possibly corrupt, but the meaning is sufficiently evident. This is a very clear statement that the generation or production of the successive levels of reality—intellect from the One, soul from intellect, the sensible cosmos from soul—is not a chronological sequence, but rather refers only to the timeless ontological dependence of each level on its superior. Cf. II.9.3, 12–14; V.8.12, 21–27. The generation in question, then, is not an act or an event but a description of this relation: to say that the One "generates" or is the "cause" of intellect, or that intellect "comes to be" from the One, means *only* that intellect depends on the One in order to be. Cf. VI.9.3, 49–52, quoted in Commentary 6, 1–8. This point contributes to the present discussion because it compels us to avoid thinking of the generation of intellect as a beginning, or of the One as first existing by itself and then generating intellect. Such misconceptions would inevitably involve attributing motion or activity to the One. Plotinus' observation here thus directs us instead toward understanding the generation of intellect as nothing but intellect's dependence on the One.

6, 22–27 *What comes to . . . way at all*: A very strong argument. If intellect came to be as a result of the One's in any sense moving, willing, inclining, or exercising any activity, then the One's first and immediate product would be not intellect but rather this motion, will, inclination, or activity, and this, rather than the One itself, would be the actual cause of intellect. Not only does this violate what is meant by the One, that is, the principle by which all things exist, but it would lead to an infinite regress: we would have to ask how the One generates this motion or will, and so *ad infinitum.* Cf. the parallel argument at V.3.12, 28–31: "[The One] did not, as it were, want intellect to be generated, so that intellect was generated with the wanting generated between it [that is, the One] and the intellect that was generated; indeed, it does not want at all, for so it would be incomplete . . . " The point that any "wanting" on the One's part would imply that the One is "incomplete" (*atelēs*) in effect restates the observation in the present treatise that if the One moves it must have an end (*telos*) beyond itself toward which it moves. To avoid an infinite regress, that which is generated must be generated by the One itself, not by any motion or activity distinct from the One itself.

Plotinus' argument thus demonstrates that there can be no distinction whatsoever between the One and the One's generation of intellect. Hence the One must be understood not as a maker or producer, which would imply a being that performs an act distinct from itself, but rather as sheer "making" or "production," what Plotinus often calls "the power of all things" (III.8,10, 1; V.1.7, 9–10; V.3.15, 33; V.4.1, 36; V.4.2, 38; VI.7.32, 31), that is, the enabling condition by which beings are beings (cf. D'Ancona 1990, 448–451; Schurmann 1982, 335). Hence it is a mistake even to ask why the One generates being, for such a question presupposes the misconception of the One as a being which acts to generate. Rather, "the One" just means the "power" by which beings are beings, and only in this sense can the One be said to cause or generate being.

6, 27–28 *How, then, and . . . as it abides?*: Again, the question is not why or even how the One generates intellect, but rather how we are to conceive intellect's derivation from the One without attributing any motion or activity to the One. Thus it is intellect's dependence on the One, not the One itself, that we are to understand in terms of the metaphors of emanation that follow.

6, 28–39 *An illumination from . . . lesser than itself*: This passage is a *locus classicus* for Plotinus' so-called "theory of emanation," which is often taken to account for the generation of all things as a necessary "outflow" from the One. But this is both a misnomer and a misconception: a misnomer, because "emanation" is not a theory but a metaphor (cf. Gerson 1994, 27); a misconception, because the metaphor does not, and is not intended to, account for the generation of all things. Rather, as the immediately preceding question indicates, the passage consists of a series of images aimed at helping us to conceptualize what Proclus will call "production by being," that is, production which involves no motion on the part of the producer, no act of producing distinct from the producer itself (see Proclus, *Commentary on Plato's Parmenides* [*In Parmenidem*] 7.1167–1168). It is never possible to begin with the One and work "downward" by explaining the production of all things from it: to do so would necessarily be to conceive the One as a being and production as a motion or activity distinct from the One itself. Rather we must always begin with intellect or being and work "upward," recognizing that intellect or being depends on the One in order to be. This and only this is the sense in which being "comes from" the One or the One "generates" being. What Plotinus offers is not a "deduction" of all things from the One by way of a "law of emanation," but rather a "reduction" of all things to the One as "the power of all things," the enabling condition by which beings are beings (cf. Halfwassen 2012, 150). Cf. 6, 8, where Plotinus says that we "refer" (*anagein*) the multiplicity of beings to the One. "Emanation" is simply a metaphor for this total existential dependence.

6, 31 *necessary*: Often associated with the misconception of emanation as a theory rather than a metaphor is the misunderstanding of its "necessity" as implying that the One is, as it were, compelled to generate or is subject to a universal law such that it "must" generate. This cannot be correct, for it again attributes generation to the One as an activity, and as the absolute first principle, the One cannot be subject to or compelled by anything. Cf. Gerson (1994, 28). What Plotinus means, rather, is that there is no possible alternative, such that the One "might not" generate being. For if the One might not generate being, then its act of generating would be distinct from the One itself, a choice, will, or motion on the part of the One, and the One would then be conditioned by a relation to its products, since the One-generating would be different from the One *simpliciter*. Since the One is not a being-which-generates, but is rather nothing but "the power of all things," the condition by which beings are beings, it does not make sense to consider the One not generating, and in this sense being "necessarily" proceeds from the One. This does not mean that the One is subject to any necessity or compulsion. See VI.8.10, 34–35: the One "is not compelled by necessity, but is itself the necessity and law of the others."

The parallel passage at V.4.1, 27–36 shows that the One, just as "the power of all things" (V.4.1, 36) is not inferior but superior to the production by choice (*prohairesin*, V.4.1, 29) that characterizes rational beings (cf. Brunner 1973, 84), which in turn is superior to the production without choice that characterizes plants and inanimate things such as fire and snow. Here Plotinus explains that the One cannot be unproductive precisely in that it is (nothing but) "the power of all things."

6, **33–34** *an image of the archetypes*: As we have seen at 3, 6–12, with regard to the relation between soul and intellect, the product is the expression or manifestation of its generator in a lower, more extended or unfolded mode of presentation and apprehension. Since the product has and is nothing that is not derived to it from its generator, the difference between them is not of content but only of mode of possession. Hence the relation of product to generator is that of image to archetype, which means that the product is the same content as the generator at a secondary, subordinate level. In scholastic terms, the relation between them is not that of univocal causation, as of offspring to parent, which are both members of the same species, but rather that of equivocal causation, as of a reflection to what is reflected: the reflection is an image of its producer, not another thing of the same kind.

6, 37–41 *And all things . . . things after it*: The One is "perfect" not in the sense of being perfected or completed, but in the sense that, unlike all beings, which depend on the One and need the unity received in or possessed by them in order to be, the One neither lacks, needs, nor receives or possesses anything at all. Cf. V.2.1, 7–8: " . . . perfect in that it seeks, possesses, and needs nothing . . . "

6, 41–43 *And the greatest . . . need of [intellect]*: Intellect "needs," or depends on, the One, as the principle in virtue of which it exists, while the One, as first principle, does not depend on intellect.

6, 43–53 *And that which . . . only by difference*: Here Plotinus describes the relation of intellect to the One as analogous to the relation of soul to intellect, discussed above at 3, 6–23.

6, 43–46 *And that which . . . is of him*: Intellect, *qua* complex and determinate, cannot be the first principle, which is therefore "greater" than intellect. But since intellect has as its content and thus is one with purely intelligible reality, intellect is the perfect, highest, and paradigmatic mode of being. As an extended, discursive presentation and apprehension of the same content, soul is a dimmer expression (*logos*) of intellect; see 3, 6–12. Hence Plotinus' analogy: as soul is to intellect, so intellect is to the One. In each case, the lower level is in greater diffusion what the higher is in greater concentration. (Cf. V.3.16, 10–16, quoted in Commentary 5, 4–5.) At the highest level of all, the One is the altogether undifferentiated containment of all things (see V.5.9, 9–10; VI.8.18, 3), and as such is beyond intelligibility and being: it is neither any one distinct being, nor being as a whole, which necessarily consists of a multiplicity of mutually distinct beings (see above, Chapters 4 and 5). Cf. V.3.15, 28–32, where Plotinus explains that the One made all things "by possessing them previously," and continues, "But it is said [that is, objected] that in that case it will be a multiplicity. But then, it possessed them thus, as not distinct [from each other]; they are distinguished in what is second, in the expression [*logōi*]," that is, in intellect. See also V.2.1, 1–2, where we are told that the One is "not all things, but all things in its own way [*ekeinōs*]." Intellect is the same content "unfolded," or differentiated, and as such is intelligible and is therefore being. In just this sense, intellect or being is not the One itself, but is the expression (*logos*) of the One.

It is not surprising that Christians such as Augustine, accustomed to thinking of the Second Person of the Trinity as the "Word" (*logos*, John 1:1) and the "image" (*eikōn*, Col. 1:15) of God, should have been tempted to find Plotinus' "three principial hypostases," or levels of reality transcendent to the sensible cosmos, parallel to their own divine Trinity, and especially to find Plotinus' eternally generated divine intellect, the *logos* and image (7, 1) of the One, parallel to their own eternally generated *Logos* of God. See, e.g., Augustine, *Confessions* 7.9. But the difference between the two is in fact profound. In post-Nicene Christian orthodoxy, the Son or Word is equal to the Father, "true God of true God": the Son is God just as the Father is God. Plotinus, on the other hand, uses the concept of *logos* to articulate rather the subordination of intellect or being, the intelligible paradigm of the cosmos, to its principle, the One, as that of which it is the differentiated expression. For Plotinus, both *logos* and image always imply subordination, not equality. Hence the mere fact that soul, intellect, and the One are all incorporeal principles, transcendent to the sensible cosmos, does not mean that they are all "God" in the same sense.

6, **46–48** *But the expression . . . may be intellect*: Soul "looks to" intellect in that, as we saw at 3, 6–17, it receives its content from intellect, in its own, lesser, discursive way. Likewise, intellect "looks to" the One in that it receives its content, in a differentiated and therefore intelligible way, from the One. See also 5, 17–19 and 7, 5–17. This "looking to" is the reversion, or turning back, of soul to intellect and of intellect to the One. It is in this turning back or active receptivity that soul constitutes itself as soul and intellect as intellect.

6, 48–49 *But it sees . . . soul and intellect*: The only difference of intellect from the One, as of soul from intellect, is in each case the lesser, more unfolded mode of possession of the same content.

6, 50–51 *Everything yearns for . . . generated are alone*: This "yearning" or "love" is yet another expression of the constitutive reversion of the lower level to its superior, that is, the dependence of the lower on the higher understood as an active, self-constituting receptivity on the part of the lower.

6, 53 *separated only by difference.* See Commentary 3, 21–23. Intellect is distinguished from the One, as soul is from intellect, only by the more unfolded mode in which the same content is possessed or received. This is why, as Plotinus says at the start of the next chapter, there is a sense in which intellect can be said to be the One, although the One is not intellect.

Chapter 7

Continued discussion of how we are to understand the derivation of intellect from the One. Intellect is constituted as the multiplicity of intelligible being by its pluralizing mode of receptivity. In this sense intellect generates its own contents, and in a different sense generates soul as subordinate to itself.

7, 1–4 *But we say . . . of the sun*: For the sense in which intellect is an image or "likeness" of the One, see Commentary 6, 33–34 and 43–46. Intellect "in a way" is the One, in that what the One encompasses without differentiation and hence in a manner beyond intelligibility and being, intellect possesses in a differentiated, intelligible way, and hence as being. Thus we may say that intellect "in a way" is the One, but not that the One is intellect, just as we may say that a reflection or a portrait of Socrates "in a way" is Socrates, but not that Socrates himself is the reflection or portrait.

7, 4–5 *But that is not intellect*: Precisely as the enfolding or undifferentiated containment of all things, the One cannot be intellect, for intellect necessarily involves differentiation: see above, 4, 39–40.

7, 5 *How then does it generate intellect?*: The question is well explained by Igal (1971, 130): "It is not so much a request for information (In what way does the One generate intellect?) as a demand for the solution of a difficulty: 'But that (=the One) is not intellect. How, then, does it generate intellect?' The meaning is: 'How can a supremely simple unity, as the One is, generate this multiple universe which intellect is?'" The solution will be given in the following lines (6–18), in terms of intellect's pluralizing mode of receptivity.

7, 5–6 *In that by . . . itself is intellect*: The interpretation of this sentence is controversial. Does it mean that the One returns toward and sees itself, and that the One's self-seeing is intellect? Or that intellect returns toward and sees the One, and that this seeing is intellect? This controversy is connected with that concerning the similar passage at 6, 18 (see Commentary 6, 17–19). Our reading follows Armstrong (*ad loc.*) and Igal (1971, 131–137) in taking the earlier passage to mean that the One is "turned toward itself" and the present passage to mean that intellect "returns to" the One, for the following reasons. First, to say that the One "returns to itself" would be to attribute motion to the One. The passage at 6, 18 is not truly parallel; see Igal (1971, 135–136). There, as we have seen,

Plotinus evidently uses the phrase "turned toward itself" to express the One's motionlessness and unrelatedness to anything. In the present passage, on the other hand, he is clearly referring to an activity, which he then specifies as an activity of seeing. Second, "seeing," or cognition of any kind, *always* implies for Plotinus a duality of the "seer" and the "seen," even in the case of intellect where what is seen is its own content and thus itself (see Commentary 4, 31–33). To attribute self-seeing to the One would therefore be to import duality into the One. Finally, to say that the One's self-seeing is intellect would in effect be to say that the One is intellect; but we have just been told in the previous sentence that the One is *not* intellect. On the other hand, to say that intellect "turns back" and "looks to" the One, and that in so doing it comes to be as intellect, is in accord with Plotinus' regular account of the two "moments" in the production of intellect, to which he has already alluded: see Commentary 5, 17. Intellect constitutes itself as the multiplicity of forms, and thus as actual intellect ("sight which sees," 5, 19), in apprehending the One according to its own, multiple, mode of possession. Thus Plotinus here recasts the question, "How does the One generate intellect?" in terms of the "seeing," the revertive or receptive activity, of intellect, rather than any activity of the One. How does intellect, as multiple, come from the One? In that it possesses, in differentiated multiplicity, as intelligible being, what occurs (*enedrame*,

V.2.1, 2) without differentiation in and as the One (cf. V.3.15, 28–32, quoted in Commentary 6, 43–46).

The meaning of Plotinus' compressed statement here is more fully laid out in a closely parallel passage in V.3: "Wherefore this intellect which is multiple, when it wishes to think the beyond, [thinks] that One itself, but wishing to intend it as simple, comes out always apprehending something else [*allo*: cf. 11, 10 in the present treatise], multiplied in itself; so that it drove toward it not as intellect, but as sight not yet seeing, and came out possessing what it itself made multiple . . . This became multiple from one, and knowing in this way it saw it, and then became seeing sight. Now [*ēdē*] it is intellect, when it possesses [this multiplicity], and possesses [it] as intellect; prior to this it is only desire and unformed sight. This intellect, then, intended that [that is, the One], but by receiving [*labōn*] became intellect . . . " (V.3.11, 1–5, 9–13). See also VI.7.15, 12–14: "[Intellect] contemplates the things contemplated, which are boniform, and these things which it possessed when it contemplated the nature of the Good. But they came to it not as they were there [that is, in the Good], but as it [that is, intellect] possessed them." But again (cf. Commentary 5, 17), we must not understand this as a sequence, as if we begin with the One, which then generates inchoate or "pre-intellect," which then turns back to the One and receives determination, thus becoming intellect proper. Phrases such as "not as intellect," "sight not yet seeing," "desire and unformed sight," and "not yet intellect" simply refer to intellect *qua* potential, receptive, and, in being receptive, pluralizing in relation to the One. Phrases such as "seeing sight" or "now it is intellect," that is, intellect proper, refer to intellect *qua* actualized by the One and possessing or knowing the multiplicity of intelligible being as its content.

The line of thought in the present passage, then, may be paraphrased as follows:

We have discovered that intellect, as multiple, is not first, but depends on the One. Objection: How can intellect, in that it is multiple, derive from the One, which is not multiple? Answer: Intellect is multiple in virtue of its properly intellectual and therefore necessarily differentiated mode of possession. Thus what is not multiple in and as the One, is multiple in and as intellect.

In this sense, just as soul is constituted as soul rather than intellect in virtue of its discursive mode of apprehension (3, 13–17), so intellect is constituted as intellect rather than the One in virtue of its intellectual mode of apprehension. In the next sentences (7, 6–19) Plotinus develops this answer more fully.

7, 6–8 *For that which . . . a line, etc.*: It makes little difference whether, as, e.g., Atkinson (1983, 160–163) argues, the text of this passage is corrupt, or, as, e.g., Igal (1971, 137–142) and Armstrong (*ad loc.*) contend, this is an

elliptical reference to an analogy well known to Plotinus'
original readers. In either case, the meaning is sufficiently
clear: "Consider sense a line, intellect a circle, the One
the center" (cf. Igal 1971, 140–141; HS$_2$ *ad loc.*). Sense is
represented by a line in that what is sensed is extrinsic
to the sensing and is received *ab extra* (see Commentary
1, 12–15). Intellect, by contrast, is represented by a circle
(cf. Plato, *Laws* 897d2–898b3) because it is self-contained,
in that what it apprehends is not extrinsic to itself. The
One, as absolutely non-plural, is represented by the center. Plotinus develops this analogy more fully at VI.8.18,
4–30. Here it becomes clear that each point of the circle,
as it were, depends from the center via a different radius,
so that what is without differentiation in and as the
center is received differently in and as each point. Thus
the many points, and hence the circle as a whole, may be
regarded as the manifestation, that is, the differentiated
expression, presentation, or image, of the center, while
the center remains undifferentiated in itself. "And it is
manifest [*emphainetai*] through the lines what sort of
thing [*hoia*] that [the center] is, as it were unfolded without
being unfolded [that is, it is unfolded *qua* circle, and not
unfolded *qua* center]. In this way we must understand
that intellect and being, having come to be from that,
and as it were poured out and unfolded and depending
from that, from its own intellectual nature bears witness
that in a way intellect is in the One without being intellect; for it is one" (VI.8.18, 17–22). In other words, all the

contents of intellect, all being, occur (V.2.1, 2) in the One without differentiation, and thus not as intellect or being. Plotinus continues, "As, there [that is, in the analogy], neither the radii nor the circle are the center, but it [the center] is the father of circle and radii, giving traces of itself and by its abiding power having generated radii and circle, not at all cut off from itself, by a certain strength; so too, that [the One] [is the father] of the intellectual power that runs around it, the archetype, as it were, of its image [*indalmatos*], intellect in one, while [the image] is as it were overcome by many and into many and on this account becomes intellect . . . " (VI.8.18, 22–28). Here again we see that intellect is constituted as intellect by its differentiated and pluralizing mode of possession of what is without differentiation in and as the One.

7, 8–9 *But the circle . . . is not so*: As Igal (1971, 142–143) and Atkinson (1983, 163) point out, *touto*, "this," must refer to the center that represents the One, not directly to the One itself. The sentence is best understood as an objection arising from the analogy of circle and center to intellect and the One: the circle is divisible, whereas the center is not; how then can the divisible circle, that is, intellect, be constituted by the apprehension of the indivisible center, that is, the One? See Igal (1971, 143–144), and Atkinson, (1983, 164). This objection in effect reiterates, in terms of the geometric analogy, the problem raised at 6, 1–8 and 7, 5. The next lines are Plotinus' reply to this objection.

7, 9–10 *Here too there . . . of all things*: Plotinus replies by explaining just where the geometric analogy breaks down. The One is not one or indivisible in the same sense as the center of a circle or a geometric point; cf. VI.9.5, 41–42: "Thus we do not, when we call it 'one' and 'indivisible,' mean as a point or a monad." Indeed, the One is not properly speaking one or simple at all (see Commentary 5, 4–5). Thus the One is not one simple being from which, impossibly, we have to explain the derivation of multiple beings. It is rather "the power of all things," that is, the enabling condition, and in that sense the productive power, by which all beings are beings (cf. Igal 1971, 146–147; Atkinson 1983, 165). As such it is "everywhere" (V.5.8–9), that is, present throughout all beings, without itself being divided. As the "power of all things," the One is seen differently in all things (see 11, 7–13) and this differentiated seeing is intellect's self-constitution as the multiplicity of intelligible being.

7, 10–11 *The things, then, . . . not be intellect*: The things of which the One is the power are the beings, or forms. These are what intellect, properly speaking, "sees," that is, knows or apprehends and thus has as its contents. Intellection, *qua* receptive, renders what it receives multiple and determinate, and thus intelligible, and as such renders them not the One itself. In this sense it "cuts them off" from the One for itself. In doing so, intellection constitutes what it receives as the multiplicity of intelligible forms and constitutes itself as intellect proper, that is, actual intellectual apprehension having as its content intelligible reality.

7, 11–15 *For, of itself . . . are from that*: The word *ēdē*, "already," indicates that this refers to intellect in its first or "pre-intellectual" moment, that is, intellect *qua* potential or receptive. As such it is an awareness, or as it were a "looking," but only potentially a "seeing," in that considered *qua* potential it does not "yet" possess its proper content, reality (cf. III.8.11, 1–8; V.3.11, 1–13, quoted in Commentary 7, 5–6; VI.7.16, 13–22). "Reality" (*ousia*) means being-as-intelligible-form, or more precisely as the multiplicity of intelligible forms. Intellect "has the power to produce reality" in that, by its pluralizing mode of receptivity or possession, it constitutes what it receives as the multiplicity of forms. Reality is thus produced in one sense by the One, as the "power" by which beings are beings, and in another sense by intellect, in virtue of its pluralizing mode of possession. See Igal (1971, 152), and Atkinson (1983, 171). Cf. VI.7.15, 18–22: "[Intellect] then had from that [that is, the One] the power to generate and to be filled with its own offspring, since he gave what he himself did not have. But from that One there are many for this [that is, for intellect]; for being unable to possess the power which it received, it broke it up and made the one [power] many, so that it might be able to bear it by parts." It is in this sense that intellect "determines being for itself." Cf. 5, 17–18. Later in this chapter, intellect as producing its own contents is represented by the myth of Cronus generating his children and swallowing them, that is, retaining them in himself. This image would be altogether out of place unless we recognize that there is a real sense in which intellect can be said to generate, or produce, the forms that are its contents.

Plotinus' account of the generation of intellect from the One, like that of soul from intellect, is thus, again, closely comparable to Proclus' doctrine of "self-constituted" terms; see Commentary 3, 13–17. Being self-constituted does not mean that the term in question is not dependent on, and in that sense made to be by, a higher level of reality. For Proclus, each term in a descending series is the same content as its prior, or cause, but in its own lesser way (see *Elements of Theology* 18 and 97). Hence its distinctness from its cause consists in its way of appropriating, possessing, and thus being that content, and this is its mode of "reversion," or turning back to its cause. In this sense, the effect is constituted *as itself*, that is, as subordinate to and distinct from its cause, by itself, and so is "self-constituted," while all its content is derived from and is found in a superior way in its cause. So, in Plotinus, intellect is constituted as the multiplicity of forms, and thus as distinct from the One, by its own intellectual and hence differentiated mode of receiving, possessing, and thus being the same content that the One is without differentiation.

7, 14–15 *and that reality . . . and from that*: Intellect is aware that reality, or the multiplicity of forms, comes from the One and is "part" of what belongs to the One in the sense that it is a partitioning or "parceling out" (Igal 1971, 155), a pluralization of what is contained without differentiation in and as the One. See V.3.11, 1–5, 9–13, quoted in Commentary 7, 5–6; V.3.15, 28–32, quoted in Commentary 6, 43–46; VI.7.15, 18–22, quoted in Commentary 7, 11–15.

7, 15–17 *it is also . . . and from that*: So far Plotinus has been describing intellect as receptive or potential. Now he adds that this potentiality is actualized by the One and so made to be intellect proper, as seeing is actualized by the seen and so made to be "sight that sees" (5, 19). Its being actualized or "perfected" is its coming to be actual intellect, having as its content, and thus being one with, intelligible reality. Thus it is "perfected into reality," that is, actualized so as to be reality. Cf. the analogous account of soul in relation to intellect at 3, 13–17. Again, the whole account is a presentation in temporal terms of the non-temporal relation of intellect to the One, as possessing in its own intellectual and hence necessarily differentiated mode, as intelligible being, what is undifferentiated in and as the One.

7, 17–18 *It sees that . . . from the undivided*: Intellect recognizes that all that it is—the act of thinking which is its life, and the forms or beings which are the contents of that act—are from the One. What is "divided," that is, differentiated, in and as intellect, is "undivided," that is, undifferentiated, in and as the One.

7, 18–19 *because he is none of all things*: All things can come from, or depend on, the One, only because the One is not any being, not included in the totality of beings or "all things" as any member thereof. Cf. V.2.1, 5–7: "Because there is nothing in [the One], for this reason all things are from it, and in order that being may be, for this reason it is not being, but the generator of it." If the One were any thing, then he would be included in the totality of beings, and so could not be the principle of that totality. Cf. V.5.6, 5–13. In order that the One may be the generator or principle of all things, he himself cannot be any or all things. "[The One], then, is not intellect, but prior to intellect; for intellect is something of beings, but that is not something, but prior to each thing, nor is it a being; for being has as it were a shape of being, but that has no shape, even intelligible shape. For since the nature of the One is generative of all things, it is none of them" (VI.9.3, 36–40). Each being, and all beings taken together, depend on the One in order to be. *Therefore* the One cannot be any being. In this sense it is only "because" the One is not any being, "none of all things," that all things can come from him.

7, 19–20 *For this is . . . by any shape*: "Shape" (*morphē*), here, means determination of any kind. Plotinus frequently uses the term *morphē* in this sense; see, e.g., VI.7.32–33; VI.9.3, 38–39. To be "confined by any shape" means to be determinate, and to be determinate is to be something, that is, some being. Hence the One can be not any being, but rather the principle of all beings, only by not being determinate.

7, 20 *For that is one only*: As the universal principle of being as such, the One is neither any "this one," any thing that has the character of unity (see Commentary 5, 6–9), nor the distinct unity *of* any being, "confined," limited, or, as later philosophers will say, "contracted" to that thing. "For to know is some one [*hen . . . ti*]; but this [that is, the One] is one without the 'some'; for if it were some one, it would not be the One itself [*autoen*]" (V.3.12, 51). "One only" is another way of saying "one without the 'some,'" that is, not the determinate or "confined" unity *of* anything.

7, 20–21 *and if it . . . among the beings*: Nor is the One all beings taken as a totality (cf. VI.9.2, 44–45; III.8.9, 40). If he were, he would be being, or that-which-is, as a whole. But since being as a whole depends on the One, the One cannot be being as a whole. The One is neither any thing nor all things, but rather the principle of all things.

7, 21–22 *For this reason . . . are from it*: The "things in intellect" are all the forms, or beings. The One is not any of these, but rather the principle that they depend on, and in that sense come from.

7, 23–26 *This indeed is . . . it possesses existence*: Along with the similar passage at V.5.6, 1–13, this is one of the clearest statements anywhere in the *Enneads* of why no being can be the first principle and the first principle cannot be any being. To be, that is, to be a being, is to be determinate, to be this definite "something," and as such to be intelligible. Thus it is by being determinate that the contents of intellect are realities, that is, intelligible beings or forms. Hence they are beings, or "possess existence," in virtue of their determination. Every being, therefore, in that it is dependent on the determination that it has, is not the first principle. Conversely, the first principle, in that it must not be dependent, cannot be a determinate "this" and so cannot be any being. Cf. VI.9.3, 36–40, quoted above in Commentary 7, 18–19.

7, 27 *"Of this lineage"*: At this point there is a marked relaxation of philosophical intensity. Having completed the closely argued ascent from soul to intellect to the One,

Plotinus now reviews his conclusions and leads us back down from the One to intellect to soul.

7, 27 [*a lineage*]: Accepting, with HS$_2$, Igal's proposed emendation of *axios* to *axias* (see Igal 1971, 156–157), so that this word ("worthy") modifies *geneas* ("lineage") rather than *nous* ("intellect").

7, 28 *none other*: Since intellect is the highest, perfect, and paradigmatic level of thought and being, there are no other levels, subordinate to the One itself, from which intellect derives. Cf. 6, 49 and 53: there is "nothing between" intellect and the One, and they are "separated only by difference."

7, 28–29 *and once it . . . beings with itself*: The sense in which intellect generates the forms, or all beings, has been discussed at length above. It generates them "with itself" in that they are not subordinate to it, like soul, but are its content and thus one with it. Hence in generating the forms, intellect constitutes itself as actual intellect.

7, 29–30 *all the beauty of the forms*: On the identification of the forms as beauty, see Commentary 4, 1–12.

7, 30 *all the intelligible gods*: Since each form is the content of a distinct act-of-thinking within the one complex act-of-thinking that is intellect, each form may be regarded as an "intelligible god." Cf. V.8.9, 14–19.

7, 30–35 *It is full . . . intellect in satiety*: For Cronus as a mythological representation of intellect, see Commentary 4, 9–10. Here Plotinus uses the grotesque myth of Cronus swallowing his offspring to illustrate the point that the intelligibles are not extrinsic to but are the contents of intellectual apprehension. These purely intelligible forms, as distinct from the sensible forms that are images of them, are not in matter, which is here mythically represented by Rhea, the mother who is not permitted to raise the offspring of Cronus. The name "Rhea" also carries connotations of Heraclitean flux (see Plato, *Cratylus* 402a8-b4), as opposed to the eternality of the forms in intellect. Cronus, retaining his offspring within himself, is "full" and is thus "intellect in satiety." *Nous en korōi* is a pun on the name Cronus; see 4, 9–10.

7, 35-37 *and after that . . . is perfect intellect*: Zeus represents soul (see Commentary 4, 9–10), which is generated by intellect in a different sense from that in which intellect generates its own contents, not as coordinate and one with itself but as a subordinate image of itself. Intellect generates the forms when it is not "yet" perfect, that is, *qua* potential and self-constitutively receptive to the One.

But it is intellect *qua* actualized, or "perfected into reality" (7, 15–17) that generates soul.

7, 38–42 *But here again . . . which generated [it]*: For the sense in which soul is lesser than and an image of intellect, see 3, 6–12. Soul receives determination from intellect, and is thus, *qua* receptive, indeterminate in relation to intellect. This reinforces Plotinus' analogy: as soul is to intellect, so intellect is to the One; see 6, 43–49.

7, 42–43 *And the offspring . . . which thinks discursively*: See 3, 6–17.

7, 43–44 *and this is . . . dependent on it*: See 3, 6–12. Soul is comparable to a "light" in the sense of an illumination proceeding from intellect (cf. 6, 28); it is a "trace" of intellect, as intellect is of the One (V.5.5, 14; VI.8.18, 15 and 23) in that it is an "outward," extended expression of the same content.

7, 44–45 *dependent on that . . . joined to that*: Here, rather exceptionally in this treatise, Plotinus uses *ekeino* with reference to intellect rather than the One. But this may be explained in terms of his analogy: as intellect is to the One, so soul is to intellect. Thus intellect is, analogously, "that" in relation to soul.

7, 44–48 *on one side . . . inferior to soul*: On the one hand, soul "looks to" or reverts toward and is informed by intellect. By doing so, it thinks: if soul did not possess in its own, lesser way, as *logoi*, the forms that are properly in intellect, it could not think at all. See 11, 1–7, and V.9.3, 30–34. But soul also animates, informs, and thus generates sensible things, and through the body it can receive impressions of sensible things. The soul makes discursive judgments regarding the sensible things by referring the impressions that it receives from "below" to the *logoi* that it receives from "above" (see V.3.2, 7–13). Plotinus adds, "We are this, the proper [part] of soul, in between two powers, a worse and a better, the worse sense, the better intellect" (V.3.3, 37–39). This "in between" status is precisely what makes possible the fall of the soul with which the present treatise began: the soul turns its attention "outward" and "downward" toward sensible things, rather than "inward" and "upward" to intellect and the One. See Commentary 12, 1–10. The end of Chapter 7 thus leads, after the doxographic interruption of Chapters 8–9, to the resumption of Plotinus' discussion of the self at the beginning of Chapter 10.

Chapter 8

These doctrines are not new, but are the teachings of Plato. Aspects of them are also found in Parmenides.

8, 1–4 *And this explains . . . around third things*: Plotinus takes these enigmatic words from Plato's (or pseudo-Plato's) *Letter* 2 as a reference to the One, intellect, and soul.

8, 4–5 *And he also . . . by "cause," intellect*: Plotinus takes the words "father of the cause" from Plato's (or pseudo-Plato's) *Letter* 6 as a reference to the One. Cf. VI.8.14, 37–38, where, alluding to the same (pseudo-)Platonic passage, Plotinus calls the One "father of reason and of cause and of causal reality." Intellect is the paradigmatic and productive cause of the sensible cosmos, but this cause itself may be said to have a "father" in that it derives from the One.

8, 5 *for his demiurge is intellect*: Plato frequently refers to the demiurge or craftsman of the cosmos, especially but not exclusively in the *Timaeus*, and identifies this demiurge as intellect (*Timaeus* 39b7, 47e4; see also *Phaedo* 97c1–4; *Philebus* 30c6–d8; *Republic* 507c7–8, 530a6; *Sophist* 265c4; *Statesman* 270a5). Plotinus regularly identifies his intellect with Plato's demiurge, in that it is the divine thinking, having as its content the intelligible forms, from which the sensible cosmos derives and of which it is the image. See 4, 1–12.

8, 6–8 *But the "father" . . . and "beyond reality"*: Plotinus identifies the "father of the cause" with the Good of the *Republic*, which is "not reality but beyond reality in seniority and power" (*Republic* 509b8–9). Plato does not expressly say that the Good is beyond intellect, but he implies as much by indicating that the Good is not truth or knowledge but is above these and is the cause of, or provides, knowledge, truth, and intellect (*Republic* 508b9–c2, 508e1–509a7, 517b8–c4). Aristotle in a lost treatise *On Prayer* is reported to have said that "god is either intellect or something beyond intellect" (fr. 49=Ross 1955, 57).

8, 8–9 *And he frequently . . . intellect as form*: For being as form or idea in Plato, see, e.g., *Republic* 507b 5–10; *Sophist* 246b6–7.

8, 10–14 *These accounts given . . . doctrines are ancient*: For Plotinus, as for late antique philosophers in general, it is important to show that his theories are not innovative but are in continuity with a tradition stretching back to Plato and beyond.

8, 14–18 *Parmenides too, earlier . . . are the same*: Plotinus is our principal source for this fragment of Parmenides (DK B 3), which he quotes or paraphrases many times: I.4.10, 6; III.5.7, 51; III.8.8, 8; V.6.6, 22–23; V.9.5, 29–30; VI.7.41, 18. (The only record of this fragment outside of Plotinus is Clement of Alexandria, *Stromateis* 6.23.) This perhaps suggests the exceptional importance of this line to Plotinus, as a testimony to the unity of intellect and being. Its precise meaning in Parmenides' poem is controversial. Today it is most often taken to mean, "The same is for thinking and for being": whatever is, can be thought, and whatever can be thought, is. Even taken in this sense, Parmenides' insight here is foundational for the entire philosophical tradition to which Plotinus belongs, as the earliest express statement of the equation of being and intelligibility. But Plotinus' stronger reading of the line, as an expression of his own doctrine of the sameness of being and intellect, can also be defended: since there can be nothing included in thinking that is not included in being, and vice versa, they coincide as regards content, and are thus "the same." For a good defense of this reading of the fragment see Henn (2003, 53–54).

8, 18–20 *And he said . . . stay the same*: Parmenides (DK B 8.3–21) denies that being is subject to change, and expresses this in a way that suggests a timeless, unextended, eternal present rather than merely unchanging duration through time: "It neither was once, nor will be, since now it is, all together, one, continuous" (DK B 8.5–6). See Commentary 4, 16–25.

8, 20–22 *and likened it . . . but within itself*: Parmenides (DK B 8.43) says that being is "like" a sphere, apparently in order to suggest its undifferentiated homogeneity and, as Plotinus here indicates, its all-inclusiveness.

8, 22–23 *But he is . . . to be many*: Despite his admiration for Parmenides, Plotinus here points out the fundamental difference between Parmenides' all-inclusive being and his own: for Parmenides, being, "since it all alike is" (DK B 8.22), is undifferentiated and therefore purely one. Plotinus, on the other hand, as we have seen, argues that there must be difference as well as sameness between intellect and being, and that, since intelligibility depends on differentiation, intelligible being as a whole must consist of a multiplicity of mutually distinct beings, or forms. And precisely because, *contra* Parmenides, being is not absolutely one, it cannot be the first principle.

8, 23–27 *But the Parmenides . . . the three natures*: Plotinus clearly recognizes the distinction between the actual or historical Parmenides and the character Parmenides in Plato's dialogue of that name. Plotinus takes the latter to be articulating his own doctrine of the three hypostases by distinguishing between "the first One," that is, the One itself, "the second one," that is, the "one-many" that Plotinus identifies as intellect, and the "third" one, the "one-and-many" that Plotinus identifies as soul. In this way Plotinus associates the One, intellect, and soul with, respectively, the first, second, and third hypotheses of Plato's *Parmenides*. This appears to be as far as he goes in this direction. Later Neoplatonists go much farther, associating the many hypotheses with different levels of reality in a variety of ways.

Chapter 9

Such doctrines are also suggested, though imprecisely, by Anaxagoras, Heraclitus, and Empedocles. Criticism of Aristotle's theories of the first principle as intellect, and of a multiplicity of such principles.

9, 1–3 *Anaxagoras, too, calling . . . of his antiquity*: According to Anaxagoras, "intellect is . . . mixed with no thing, but alone itself in itself" (DK B 12). Anaxagoras' idea of intellect as the ordering principle of the cosmos is an important precursor to Plato's divine, demiurgic intellect, Aristotle's unmoved mover, and Plotinus' paradigmatic intellect. See Plato, *Phaedo* 97b8–c2; Aristotle, *Metaphysics* 1.3.984b15–19. Anaxagoras, however, does not offer a doctrine of the One beyond intellect. Thus Plotinus seems to be implying that Anaxagoras was right to regard the first principle as "simple" and "separate" in the sense that it is not material or sensible, but "imprecise" in that he failed to recognize, or at least to say clearly, that intellect, although it is "separate," "pure," and "unmixed" with matter, is not absolutely simple, and hence is not the supreme first principle.

9, 3–5 *And Heraclitus knows . . . being and "flowing"*: Heraclitus' famous doctrine that "all things flow" (see Diogenes Laertius, *Lives of Eminent Philosophers* 9.1.8) is discussed at length by Plato, notably at *Theaetetus* 152d2–e9, 179d6–183b5 and *Cratylus* 402a4–c3, 439b10–440e2, where Plato contrasts these "flowing" things with changeless forms. Aristotle (*Metaphysics* 1.6.987a33–b10) reports that this Heraclitean view of sensible things was one of the sources for Plato's distinction between changing sensible things and changeless intelligible forms. Plotinus takes Heraclitus' doctrine of flux as a recognition that bodies are always undergoing generation and corruption, and then, rightly or wrongly, credits Heraclitus with positing a higher principle which is one, eternal, and intelligible. For Plotinus, of course, eternal intelligible being is not absolutely one, and the One is not, properly speaking, either eternal or intelligible, for these are attributes of being, not of the One. But in the present context "eternal and intelligible" evidently simply means "not changeable and sensible." Thus Plotinus finds in Heraclitus another "imprecise" precursor of his own doctrine.

9, 5–7 *And for Empedocles . . . elements as matter*: Aristotle, *Metaphysics* 12.10. 1075b3, says that according to Empedocles love is the Good, which for Plotinus is the same as the One. Plotinus assumes that for Empedocles this force is incorporeal, as distinct from the elements on which it acts and which thus hold the place of "matter." Cf. Aristotle, *Metaphysics* 1.8.989a20–21.

9, 7–27 *Aristotle, later, takes . . . not separate them?*: This entire passage is a brief but incisive criticism of Aristotle's theory of the unmoved mover or movers. Plotinus first briefly observes that Aristotle's doctrine that the unmoved mover "thinks itself" implies that it is complex and hence cannot be the absolute first principle. He then argues at greater length that Aristotle's theory of a multiplicity of unmoved movers must either fall into incoherence or be completed by the subordination of the multiplicity of intelligibles to a higher principle which alone is truly first.

9, 7–8 *Aristotle, later, takes . . . separate, and intelligible*: Aristotle's unmoved mover, the divine intellect which is the principle on which "the universe and nature depend" (*Metaphysics* 12.7.1072b14), is "separated from sensible things" (*Metaphysics* 12.7.1073a4–5; cf. *Metaphysics* 7.17.1041a9) in that, unlike all moving or changeable things, it involves no matter (*Metaphysics* 12.6.1071b21–22; 12.8.1074a36).

9, 8–9 *but by saying . . . it not first*: A reference to Plotinus' regular argument, most fully developed in V.6 and VI.7.37–41, but also given in the present treatise at 4, 31–33, 37–39, that that which thinks, even if it thinks itself rather than anything extrinsic to itself, cannot be absolutely simple and therefore cannot be the first principle. This is his principal objection to the Aristotelian doctrine that the first principle is intellect.

9, 9–11 *And in affirming... may move one*: This refers to the theory, developed in Aristotle's *Metaphysics* 12.8.1073a14–b18, that there must be as many unmoved movers as there are celestial spheres, since each sphere must have its own mover.

9, 11–12 *he speaks with ... way from Plato*: Plato nowhere posits a definite number of intelligible beings, or forms, on the basis of any observed sensible phenomena such as the motions of the heavens. Elsewhere (VI.7.8–11), Plotinus explains that the multiplicity of forms is the result of the internal self-deployment of intellect as all the different possibilities of thought; it is not deduced from observation of the sensible world. See Commentary 4, 43.

9, 12–15 *But one might ... [principle], the first*: Plotinus points out that it is hardly reasonable to posit an independent, equally primary mover for each several sphere. Rather, since all the spheres together constitute one complex system, there must be one principle for this system as a whole. If each sphere has its own mover, therefore, none of these movers can be the first principle, and the first principle must be superior to each and all of them.

9, 15–16 *One might inquire . . . among the intelligibles*:
Aristotle posits one "first" unmoved mover (*Metaphysics*
12.7.1072a23–26, 1072b14, 1074a36–38) and argues that
there must be a single principle for the cosmos as a whole
(*Metaphysics* 12.10.1076a3–5). But he also posits a multiplicity of unmoved movers to account for the motions of
the many celestial spheres, and offers no clear explanation
of how the many movers are related to the first mover.

9, 17–23 *And if they . . . true things there*: If, for Aristotle,
the many movers come from a single first principle, then
the multiplicity of intelligibles will be a unified, complex
system, an intelligible cosmos, as in Plotinus' own account
of intelligible reality, rather than an incoherent, discon-
nected multiplicity of mutually independent principles.

9, 23–25 *But if each . . . the whole universe?*: If, on the other
hand, the many unmoved movers do not derive from a
higher, unifying principle, then they will not constitute a
single system, and the sensible universe of which they are
the movers will not be a single ordered whole, a cosmos.
Since the universe is such a whole, its moving principles
must be a coordinated, not a "random" multiplicity.

9, 25–26 *And how can . . . intelligibles, the movers?*: The force
of this objection is somewhat obscure. Perhaps Plotinus'
point is simply that there is no evident necessity to posit
a one-to-one relation of spheres and intelligible movers,

as Aristotle does (somewhat tentatively) at *Metaphysics* 12.8.1074a15–17.

9, 26–27 *And how can . . . to separate them?*: Another classic objection to a multiplicity of unmoved movers. Aristotle argues that as pure actuality the unmoved movers are without matter (*Metaphysics* 14.2.1088b14–28). For Plotinus, this raises the problem of how they are differentiated from one another. Within his own system, Plotinus infers from the plurality of forms something in the intelligible analogous to matter: the indeterminate dyad or "the matter there" (II.4.4, 2–7, 14–17; see above, Commentary 5, 6–9 and 14–17). In Plotinus' thought, there cannot be a multiplicity of pure actualities. Any multiplicity necessarily depends on a higher unity and therefore involves an aspect of receptivity or potentiality, and thus in some sense matter. For an Aristotelian response to this objection, arguing that Aristotle's system has no need for a principle of differentiation among pure forms, see Owens (1978, 448–450, 458–460).

9, 28–32 *Thus, those of . . . it alone altogether*: Those, including Plato, who posit the One as the first principle, do so in accordance with what Plotinus regards as the doctrine of Pythagoras. Pherecydes (DK A 4) was reputedly a teacher of Pythagoras.

Chapter 10

The One, intellect, and soul must be recognized in ourselves, as transcendent levels of the self. The first of these, in ascending order, is rational soul.

10, 1–4 *It has now . . . nature of soul*: This briefly summarizes what was worked out at length in chapters 2–7.

10, 5–10 *And just as . . . "the inner man"*: Soul, intellect, and the One are found in each person, but in that they are supersensible, incorporeal principles, they do not pertain to the sensible aspects of the person. They are, metaphorically, "outside," in the sense of transcendent to, all that is sensible. In that they are "deeper" or more fundamental levels of the self than the outwardly visible body, they may also be called the "inner" man. Thus we may say that the "inner" man is transcendent to and in that sense "above" or "outside of" the "outer" man. In the interplay and interchangeability between "outer" and "inner" as metaphors for transcendence (itself a spatial metaphor, literally "rising past"), Plotinus clearly shows his awareness of the metaphorical nature and inadequacy of all such spatial expressions.

10, 10–12 *Our soul, then . . . nature of soul*: On the relation between our soul and soul in general, see Chapter 2.

10, 12 *And it is perfect in possessing intellect*: See Chapter 3: the soul's perfection, completion, or actualization lies in its possessing, in its own, subordinate way, the same intelligible contents that intellect has in a superior way.

10, 12–13 *There is intellect . . . that provides reasoning*: "Intellect that reasons" is the soul's discursive reasoning power (see Commentary 3, 12–13); "intellect that provides reasoning" is intellect proper, the non-discursive intellectual apprehension which is one with the intelligible reality that it knows. Intellect in the latter sense "provides" the soul's reasoning in that it is the condition for the possibility of discursive reasoning at the level of soul. Plotinus develops this point more fully in Chapter 11.

10, 13–17 *Now, that in . . . mixed with body*: Plato in the *Phaedo* (65b9–67d2, 79c2–d7, 83a3–b4) argues that since "the reality of . . . things" (65d13) is not sensible but intelligible, the soul cannot know this reality "through the body" (65e1, 79c5), that is, "by means of sense" (79c5), but rather "by itself" or "itself by itself" (65c7, 65d1–2, 66a1–2,

66e1, 67c7, 79d1, 79d4, 83b1), by "pure thought" (66a2) and in this sense by "purifying" or "separating" itself from the body (67a5–6, 67c5–d2). Likewise Aristotle argues that the human soul's intellectual power, in order that it may be able to know, to possess, and thus to become all the intelligibles, must have no positive nature of its own and therefore, unlike all other faculties of the soul, cannot be the actuality of any bodily organ. Thus he repeatedly indicates that intellect, unlike the rest of the soul, is separate from and unmixed with the body. See Commentary 2, 45–47. Plotinus here follows both Plato and Aristotle. The general point is that reason, as the apprehension at some level of what is intelligible, cannot be a corporeal activity, and hence that the soul *qua* rational must be "separate," that is, "not mixed with body." Cf. Commentary 1, 30–35 and 2, 45–47.

10, 17–18 *one would not . . . the first intelligible*: "First," that is, in the ascending series: the soul's reasoning, as the lowest level of thinking, is the first or lowest level of the self and of reality that transcends the body.

10, 18–24 *For thus it . . . in the head*: Again Plotinus expresses his awareness of the metaphorical nature of terms such as "separate" and "above." The reasoning power is not spatially separate from, outside of, or above the body, but is altogether incorporeal and non-spatial.

10, 24–27 *And his exhortation . . . from the body*: Plotinus recognizes that when Plato insists that we must "separate" the soul from the body (e.g., *Phaedo* 64c4–67d2), this does not mean either spatial separation or even simply metaphysical distinctness, since the soul is "by nature" an incorporeal reality and in that sense always already "separate" from body. Plotinus explains that Plato's exhortation is rather to reorient our attention, our cognition and desire, away from sensible things that we encounter by means of the bodily sense-organs, and from the sensory images derived from these things, toward incorporeal, intelligible reality. "Being separate" is thus a cognitive, ethical, and spiritual condition, not a "going elsewhere." At I.8.6, 10–12, Plotinus cites *Theaetetus* 176a8–b2 and explains that "'flight' means not departing from earth but being on earth 'just and holy with wisdom.'" To "be separate" means not to go elsewhere but to live a life of virtue and intellectual contemplation "on earth."

10, 27–31 *if somehow one . . . concern with it*: In many places Plotinus addresses the problem of the relation between the "higher" soul, or soul *qua* rational, and the "lower" soul, or soul *qua* informing and animating the body. These "parts" of the soul must not be understood as, so to speak, two different "pieces," but rather as different functions or powers of one soul; on this point see II.9.2, 6, "One nature in many powers," and Atkinson (1983, 227). How then does the conversion and purification of the higher power, its orientation toward intellect and intelligible reality, affect the lower? As we have seen (Commentary 1, 3–17), the rational soul's being contemplative enables it to govern the body in such a way that the body belongs to the soul rather than the soul to the body, as the world-soul and the souls of the stars animate their bodies. At I.1.3, 21–25, in a passage closely parallel to the present one, Plotinus explains, "I mean that one [part] is separated, that which uses [the body], but the other [part] is somehow mixed [with the body] and is itself on a level with what it uses; so that philosophy turns back even the latter toward that which uses and leads that which uses away, as far as it is not altogether necessary, from that which it uses . . . " Elsewhere Plotinus argues that the purified soul "will want to make the irrational [part], too, pure, so that it may not be battered; or, if it is, its shocks will be few and straightway undone by its neighborhood; as if someone who is a neighbor to a wise man should benefit from the wise man's neighborhood, either becoming like [him] or being ashamed so as not to dare to do anything that the good man would not wish" (I.2.5, 22–27). The general principle is that the higher aspect of soul, in being turned "upward," does not abandon but rather illuminates and perfects the lower, and in that sense may be said to "lead up" the lower aspect as well. A person whose attention and desire is oriented toward intelligible reality will not be troubled by the passions of the body.

Chapter 11

Intellect must also be present in us, as the condition for the possibility of soul's reasoning, and the One in turn must be in us, as the principle of intellect.

11, 1 *Since, then, there is soul*: That is, there is such soul within us; see below, 6.

11, 1–4 *soul which reasons . . . [level of] soul*: In the present context, "justice" and "beauty" simply serve as stock Platonic examples of forms. See, e.g., *Phaedo* 65d4–7; *Republic* 475e9–476a4, 479e1–3. Plotinus' argument, expressed here very elliptically, is what is called in Kantian terms a transcendental argument, in that it is an argument from the phenomenon of discursive judgment to the condition for the possibility of such judgment. It is possible to judge that a particular act (or law, institution, etc.) is just or unjust, or even meaningfully to inquire whether it is just or unjust, only if there is a standard,

173

justice itself, in relation to which the act may be judged. The standard itself must be "stable," that is, changeless, in order to serve as the standard for all such judgments. Our capacity to make such judgments and inquiries shows that we must in some sense possess, know, or have this changeless standard within ourselves. In this sense the soul's reasoning "comes from," that is, depends on, such standards. This is in fact the real force of Plato's myth of recollection: our capacity to make judgments regarding sensible particulars indicates the presence within us of the intelligible standards for these judgments, so that, as Plato concludes, intelligible reality "is ours" (*Phaedo* 76e1), or "the truth of beings is always in the soul" (*Meno* 86b1–2).

This is an argument that Augustine repeatedly adopts and thematizes: the rational soul's ability to judge sensible things reveals the presence within it of an immutable standard of judgment as the condition for the possibility of such judgments. See, e.g., *Of True Religion* (*De vera religione*) 30.54–31.57; *On Free Will* (*De libero arbitrio*) 2.16.41; *Confessions* 7.10 (where the phrase *vocem tuam de excelso* echoes the final words of the present treatise) and 7.17. For Augustine, however, this standard, *qua* intelligible and immutable, is God. Plotinus, on the other hand, argues that it is necessary to look still higher than such standards to the One, as the condition or principle of their existence. Cf. Brunner (1973, 95).

11, 4–7 *And if soul . . . always possesses justice*: Again, the human soul's intermittent reasoning depends on an abiding, non-discursive, intellectual knowledge of standards such as justice. Thus it is only the presence in us of intellect, that is, the knowledge of intelligible reality which is one with intelligible reality itself, that makes our intermittent discursive reasoning possible. To "possess justice," in this context, does not mean "to be just," but rather to know the form justice.

11, 7 *and there must . . . god of intellect*: A continuation and extension of the transcendental argument: just as intellect must be in us as the enabling condition for reasoning, so the One must be in us as the enabling condition for intellect.

Some translators (e.g., Harder, Igal) prefer to read, "the principle and cause of intellect, God." But Plotinus' phrasing, consisting of three parallel terms linked by repeated *kai*, does not suggest this. The One is the "god of intellect" in that it is the principle, transcendent or superior to intellect, in virtue of which intellect exists and to which intellect turns.

11, 7–10 *Not being divided . . . him, as other*: Both the construction and the sense are problematic. The meaning, however, would appear to be this: as the condition for the existence of anything at any level, the One may be

"seen," or contemplated, in many things, indeed in each
and every thing. Even a mere aggregate, like a flock, must
have some unity, must be *one* flock, in order to exist as
a flock at all (VI.9.1, 1–6). Wherever there is any being
whatsoever, there the One may be seen, as the principle
for the existence of anything and everything (V.5.8, 23–9,
23). In that sense, the principle is "received" in each and
every thing. But *qua* received, it is limited to and by that
recipient. Here again we encounter the principle of reception according to the capacity of the recipient. Thus the
"one" as seen in any given thing is not "the One itself"
(*autoen*, V.3.12, 51), while the latter is not "some one," that
is, the participated unity in or of some thing, but is rather
"one without the 'some'" (V.3.12, 51; see Commentary 7,
20). Hence the One may be seen, or contemplated, in all
things, yet never as "the One itself" but only, as Plotinus
here says, "as other," that is, other than the One itself; cf.
V.3.11, 3, quoted in Commentary 7, 5–6. For this reading of *hoion allon auton*, see Atkinson (1983, 235–236). If
this interpretation is correct, it is a striking anticipation
of Proclus' distinction between the henads, that is, the
participated unities of beings, which are knowable from
their participants, and the unparticipated and hence altogether unknowable "One itself." See Proclus, *Elements of
Theology* 116 and 123; cf. Brunner (1973, 95–96).

Many translators and interpreters take the phrase
hoion allon auton to mean rather "as another self"

(Armstrong, Harder, Igal, O'Daly [1973, 90], Brunner [1973, 95]), perhaps alluding to Aristotle's description of a friend as "another self" (*allos autos*: Aristotle, *Nicomachean Ethics* 9.4.1166a31–32). This reading is possible and at first glance attractive, but upon closer examination makes little sense either contextually or metaphysically. First, as Atkinson (1983, 235) observes, Plotinus is here discussing the contemplation of the One "in many things," not in the human person in particular. Second, even in us, the One is found not as "another self," but as the inmost center or ground of the self.

11, 10–13 *as the center . . . proper to each*: Cf. the analogy of circle and center at 7, 6–8. In the present context, Plotinus' meaning is that each point on the circle is not the center itself, but is a "trace" of it, as he explains in the more extended deployment of this metaphor at VI.8.18, 4–30, quoted in Commentary 7, 6–8. That is, each point may be regarded as a differentiated presence of the common center, which in itself is undifferentiated. Thus the center may be "seen" or contemplated differently in or as each of the points, while each point, *qua* differentiated, is not the center itself.

11, 13–15 *For by such . . . are established there*: As the principle of intellect, which itself is the condition for discursive reasoning, the One is thus in us as a "center" from which all other aspects of the self depend. What we must do, therefore, is re-direct our attention toward and so establish ourselves in this inmost center of the self, without which we could neither think nor live nor be at all (see I.6.7, 11–12).

Chapter 12

We are not usually aware of these higher principles within ourselves, because we are not the higher, rational part of soul alone, but the lower levels as well. To be aware of the higher principles, we must turn our attention inward, away from sensible things.

12, 1–10 *How then, since . . . the whole soul*: This passage raises in acute form the problem of the multiple self to which Plotinus repeatedly returns. "But we—who are we?" (VI.4.14, 16). "We," or the self, in one sense, include so much that "we," in another sense, are unaware of.

In the broadest sense of the self, soul (itself involving multiple levels), intellect, and even the One, are not only metaphysical principles or levels of reality but "levels of the self" (Hadot 1993, 27). They are not an "objective" scale of entities to be climbed by a self which is another entity extrinsic to them and which remains untransformed as it passes from one level to another. Rather, the self, we may say, is whatever level it attains: at the level of intellect, we are intellect (I.1.13, 7–8; V.3.4, 10–12; V.8.10, 35–41); at the level of the One, we do not behold or join with the One from outside, but rather discover the One as the self and the self as the One (VI.9.9, 55–58; VI.9.10, 11–21; VI.9.11, 4–7). Thus the present treatise leads us to discover soul in its true rational nature, intellect, and the One, within ourselves, as higher levels of ourselves.

In a narrower sense, although intellect and the One are "in" us (10, 6), "we" are rational soul animating a body. Even in this sense, however, the self involves a multiplicity of levels: "We are many" (I.1.9, 7). In I.1 and elsewhere, Plotinus develops what we may somewhat misleadingly call a "dualistic" account of the human person. This is not the simplistic or Cartesian dualism of soul (or mind) and body, but rather the duality between higher, rational soul, which as we have seen involves no bodily organ in its activity of thinking (2, 45–47; 10, 13–17), and the composite of lower soul and body, together constituting "the living thing" or "the beast." This is closely comparable to Aristotle's distinction between the soul's intellectual faculty, which is purely incorporeal and involves no bodily organ, and "the composite," that is, the hylomorphic composite of all the soul's lesser powers and the body (see Commentary 2, 45–47 and 10, 13–17). Plotinus observes, "'We' is used in two senses, either including the beast [that is, the animal composite of soul and body] or with reference to what is already above this [that is, the higher, rational soul]" (I.1.10,

5–6). He then explains that the latter alone is "the true man" (I.1.10, 7). Elsewhere, likewise, he argues that "we" are, properly speaking, only the higher soul, and refers to the animal composite as "another man" who has become attached to us (VI.4.14, 23). Thus he arrives at an even narrower understanding of the self as the rational soul alone; cf. 2, 44–47, 49–51.

But Plotinus finds it necessary to make a further distinction within the soul. On the one hand, the rational soul must include an undescended aspect, a "part" that remains in contemplation of intelligible reality. Without this, we would have no access to the forms and so could not think at all (e.g., IV.8.4, 30–31; IV.8.8, 1–6). On the other hand, there must also be a part that is capable of reason but is not always or necessarily rational. For no division of the soul into "rational" and "non-rational" parts can explain how one and the same soul may be either "fallen," turned toward outward, sensible things, or converted, turned toward the divine principles within it: there would always be one part that is necessarily turned downward and hence unsalvageable, and another part that remains undescended and hence not in need of salvation. There must, then, be something in us that can turn in either direction, toward the higher levels within ourselves or toward the body and sensible things perceived through it. It is precisely this, as we see at the beginning of the present treatise and again here, that is oblivious and ignorant of its divine origin and its own true nature. Plotinus calls this the "middle" part, in between the undescended soul on the one hand and the lower soul that, together with the body, constitutes "the beast" on the other. "One [aspect] of our soul holds to these things [that is, intelligible beings], another to those [that is, sensibles], another [is] in between these; for since [the soul] is one nature in many powers, sometimes the whole of it is borne along to the best of it and of being, sometimes what is worse of it is dragged down and drags the middle with it . . . " (II.9.2, 4–9). Precisely as that which can turn either way, this middle part is "we" in the most decisive sense of all: "We are this, the proper [part] of soul, in between two powers, a worse and a better, the worse sense, the better intellect" (V.3.3, 37–40). The lower levels of soul are sub-rational, comprising only the sensitive, appetitive, and vegetative functions; the higher level is purely and necessarily intellectual and contemplative. The middle part, the human soul that is capable of rationality but does not always or necessarily exercise this capacity, is the "we" to which Plotinus is referring in the present passage.

12, 3–5 *They are always . . . in this state*: Intellect, the One, and the purely rational, undescended soul must always be present and at work within us; otherwise we could not think (and without the One, we could not be) at all.

12, 5–10 *For not everything . . . the whole soul*: The higher levels of reality and of the self enter into our awareness, and in that sense reach "us" (line 6), only if the middle part that can turn in either direction actively attends to (lines 14–15) and thus consciously apprehends them (cf. I.1.11, 2–8; IV.8.8, 6–9). Without this active apprehension, "we do not know" the superior levels within us, because "we" are not only or even primarily the highest, undescended part of the soul, but are rather "the whole soul," including the middle and lower levels.

12, 10–15 *And further, each . . . what is there*: Here Plotinus explains more fully that awareness or recognition of the higher principles present within us demands an active apprehension (*antilēpsis*) of them, and hence a positive "turning" (*epistrephein*) of our attention (*prosochē*) to them. To see what is there to be seen, we must look; to hear what is there to be heard, we must listen. And this explains how it can be that, although the higher principles are always present and active within us, we remain unaware of them. The failure to attend, to "look" or "listen," is precisely the "being oblivious" (1, 1) with which the treatise began.

12, 15–21 *Just as, if . . . voices from above*: Plotinus concludes with a vivid metaphor for the act of attending to that which is always within us but which we ordinarily neglect. His use of auditory rather than the more frequent visual imagery is striking although by no means isolated; cf., e.g., III.8.9, 26–28.

12, 18–19 *except as far as necessary*: Plotinus acknowledges our need for sense-perception but points out that this can be kept to a necessary minimum, so that the soul can as far as possible attend to "the voices from above" (line 21) which, we must remember, resound *within* the soul itself, in that they are not received from outside, by way of sense. A glimpse of what this attentive life might look like may perhaps be found in Porphyry's description of Plotinus himself: "He was thus at once together with [*synēn*] himself and with others, and never relaxed his attention [*prosochēn*] to himself, or only in sleep, which scantiness of food—for often he did not even take bread—and his perpetual turning [*epistrophē*] toward intellect shook off" (VP 8, 19–23).

12, 19–20 *power of apprehension pure*: This serves as a reminder that the inward turning of the soul's power of apprehension is at once and without distinction cognitive and ethical. An "impure" soul (I.6.5, 33), whose desires are directed toward sensible things, necessarily has its cognitive awareness, its attention, oriented "out and down and to the dark" (I.6.5, 38–39), rather than in and up and to the light.

Select Bibliography

I. Ancient Authors

ARISTOTLE: Bywater, L., ed. 1894. *Aristotle: Nicomachean Ethics*. Oxford: Oxford University Press.

ARISTOTLE: Ross, W. D., ed. 1924. *Aristotle: Metaphysics.* Oxford: Oxford University Press.

ARISTOTLE: Minio-Paluello, L., ed. 1949. *Aristotle: On Interpretation.* Oxford: Oxford University Press.

ARISTOTLE: Ross, W. D., ed. 1955. *Aristotle: Selected Fragments*. Oxford: Oxford University Press.

ARISTOTLE: Ross, W. D., ed. 1956. *Aristotle: On the Soul.* Oxford: Oxford University Press.

ARISTOTLE: Ross, W. D., ed. 1956. *Aristotle: Physics.* Oxford: Oxford University Press.

DIOGENES LAERTIUS: Dorandi, T., ed. 2013. *Lives of Eminent Philosophers.* Cambridge: Cambridge University Press. English trans. R. D. Hicks. 1925, repr. 1991. 2 vols. Cambridge, MA: Harvard University Press.

Die Fragmente der Vorsokratiker. Hermann Diels and Walther Kranz, eds. 1954. 7th ed. 3 vols. Berlin: Weidmannsche.

PLATO: Burnet, J., ed. 1900–1907. *Works.* 5 vols. Oxford: Oxford University Press.

PROCLUS: Steel, C., ed. 2007–2009. *Commentary on Plato's* Parmenides. 3 vols. Oxford: Oxford University Press. English trans. Glenn R. Morrow and John M. Dillon. 1987. Princeton: Princeton University Press.

PROCLUS: Dodds, E. R., ed and trans. 1963. *The Elements of Theology.* 2nd ed. Oxford: Oxford University Press.

SEXTUS EMPIRICUS: Bury, R. G., trans. 1933–1949. *Outlines of Pyrrhonism. Against the Professors.* 4 vols. Cambridge, MA: Harvard University Press. Vol. 3 contains the two books called *Against the Physicists*, also known as books 9 and 10 of *Against the Professors.*

Stoicorum Veterum Fragmenta. Von Arnim, J., ed. 1968. 4 vols. Stuttgart: Teubner.

XENOCRATES: Heinze, R. 1965. *Xenokrates: Darstellung der Lehre und Sammlung der Fragmente.* Hildesheim: Georg Olms.

II. Editions and Translations of the *Enneads*

Armstrong, A. H. 1966–1988. *Plotinus*. Greek Text with English translation and introductions. 7 vols. Cambridge MA: Harvard University Press.

Brisson, L., and J.-F. Pradeau. 2002–2010. *Plotin. Traités*. French translation and commentary. 8 vols. Paris: Flammarion. Vol. 2 contains treatises 7–21, with a translation and commentary on V.1 [10] by Francesco Fronterotta.

Harder, R., R. Beutler, and W. Theiler. 1956–1971. *Plotins Schriften*. Greek text with German translation and notes. 12 vols. Hamburg: Felix Meiner Verlag. Vol. 1a contains treatises 1–21, and vol. 1b contains notes on these treatises.

Henry, P., and H.-R. Schwyzer. (HS$_1$). 1951–1973. *Plotini Opera* I–III (editio maior). Paris and Leiden: Desclée de Brouwer and Brill.

———. (HS$_2$). 1964–1982. *Plotini Opera* I–III (editio minor, with revised text). Oxford: Oxford University Press.

Igal, J. 1982–1998. *Enéades*. 3 vols. Madrid: Editorial Gredos.

MacKenna, S. 1992. *Plotinus. The Enneads*. Burdett, NY: Larson Publications.

III. Studies on V.1 and Related Works

Armstrong, A. H. 1967. "Plotinus." In *The Cambridge History of Later Greek and Early Medieval Philosophy*, edited by A. H. Armstrong, 195–263. Cambridge: Cambridge University Press.

Atkinson, Michael. 1983. *Ennead V.1: On the Three Principal Hypostases: A Commentary with Translation.* Oxford: Oxford University Press.

Baladi, N. 1970. *La Pensée de Plotin*. Paris: Presses Universitaires de France.

Brunner, Fernand. 1973. "Le premier traité de la cinquième Ennéade: Des trois hypostases principielles." In *Etudes néoplatonicienne*, 61–98. Neufchâtel: Editions de la Baconnière.

D'Ancona, Cristina. 1990. "Determinazione e indeterminazione nel sovrasensibile secondo Plotino." *Rivista di storia della filosofia* 3: 437–474.

Deck, John. 1991. *Nature, Contemplation, and the One: A Study in the Philosophy of Plotinus*. Burdett, NY: Larson Publications.

Dillon, John. 2003. *The Heirs of Plato: A Study of the Old Academy (347–274 BC)*. Oxford: Oxford University Press.

Dodds, E. R. 1963. *Proclus. The Elements of Theology: A Revised Text with Translation, Introduction, and Commentary.* 2nd ed. Oxford: Oxford University Press.

Dorter, Kenneth. 1972. "Equality, Recollection, and Purification." *Phronesis* 17: 198–218.

Gerson, Lloyd P. 2005. *Aristotle and Other Platonists.* Ithaca: Cornell University Press.

———. 2006. "The 'Holy Solemnity' of Forms and the Platonic Interpretation of *Sophist.*" *Ancient Philosophy* 26: 291–304.

Hadot, Pierre. 1963. Review of HS₁, vol. 2. *Revue de l'Histoire des Religions* 164: 92–96.

Halfwassen, Jens. 2012. "Monism and Dualism in Plato's Doctrine of Principles." In *The Other Plato*, edited by Dmitri Nikulin, 143–159. Albany: State University of New York Press. Originally published in *Graduate Faculty Philosophy Journal* 23 (2002): 125–144.

Henn, Martin. 2003. *Parmenides of Elea.* Westport, CT: Praeger.

Igal, J. 1971. "La génesis de la inteligencia en un Pasaje de las Enéadas de Plotino (V 1.7.4–35)." *Emerita* 39: 129–157.

Klein, Jacob. 1968. *Greek Mathematical Thought and the Origin of Algebra.* Trans. Eva Brann. Cambridge and London: M.I.T. Press.

Majumdar, Deepa. 2007. *Plotinus on the Appearance of Time and the World of Sense: A Pantomime.* Aldershot: Ashgate.

Nikulin, Dmitri. 2012. "Plato: *Testimonia et Fragmenta*." In *The Other Plato*, edited by Dmitri Nikulin, 1–38. Albany: State University of New York Press.

Owens, Joseph. 1978. *The Doctrine of Being in the Aristotelian* Metaphysics. 3rd ed. Toronto: Pontifical Institute of Mediaeval Studies.

Perl, Eric D. 2014. *Thinking Being: Introduction to Metaphysics in the Classical Tradition*. Leiden and Boston: Brill.

Rist, John. 1962. "The Indefinite Dyad and Intelligible Matter in Plotinus." *Classical Quarterly* 12: 99–107.

———. 1965. "Monism. Plotinus and Some Predecessors." *Harvard Studies in Classical Philology* 70: 329–344.

Schürmann, Reiner. 1982. "L'hénologie comme dépassement de la métaphysique." *Les études philosophiques* 3: 331–350.

Torchia, N. Joseph. 1992. *Plotinus,* Tolma, *and the Descent of Being*. New York: Peter Lang.

IV. General Publications

Alt, K. 1993. *Weltflucht und Weltbejahung. Zur Frage des Leib-Seele Dualismus bei Plutarch, Numenius, Plotin*. Stuttgart: Franz Steiner Verlag.

Armstrong, A. H. 1940. *The Architecture of the Intelligible Universe in the Philosophy of Plotinus*. Cambridge: Cambridge University Press.

———, ed. 1967. *The Cambridge History of Later Greek and Early Medieval Philosophy.* Cambridge: Cambridge University Press.

Arnou, R. 1968. *Le Désir de Dieu dans la philosophie de Plotin.* 2nd ed. Rome: Presses de l'Université Grégorienne.

Dillon, J. 1977/1996. *The Middle Platonists: A Study of Platonism, 80 B.C.–A.D. 220,* London: Duckworth, 1977, 1996.

Dodds, Eric R. 1965. *Pagan and Christian in an Age of Anxiety: Some Aspects of Religious Experience from Marcus Aurelius to Constantine.* Cambridge: Cambridge University Press.

Emilsson, E. K. 1988. *Plotinus on Sense-Perception.* Cambridge: Cambridge University Press.

———. 2007. *Plotinus on Intellect.* Oxford: The Clarendon Press.

Gatti, M. L. 1996. *Plotino e la metafisica della contemplazione,* Milan: Vita e Pensiero.

Gerson, L. P. 1994. *Plotinus,* London/New York: Routledge.

———, ed. 1996. *The Cambridge Companion to Plotinus,* Cambridge: Cambridge University Press.

———, ed. 2010. *The Cambridge History of Philosophy in Late Antiquity.* 2 vols. Cambridge: Cambridge University Press.

Gottschalk, H. B. 1980. *Heraclides of Pontus*, Oxford: Oxford University Press.

Guthrie, W. K. C. 1967–1978. *A History of Greek Philosophy*, 5 vols., Cambridge: Cambridge University Press.

Hadot, Pierre. 1993. *Plotinus on the Simplicity of Vision.* Translated by M. Chase. Chicago: Chicago University Press.

Inge, W. R. 1948. *The Philosophy of Plotinus.* 3rd ed. London: Longmans, Green.

Les Sources de Plotin, 1960. Entretiens Fondation Hardt V. Vandoeuvres-Genève.

Lloyd, Anthony C. 1990. *The Anatomy of Neoplatonism.* Oxford: Clarendon Press.

Meijer, P. A. 1992. *Plotinus on the Good or the One (Enneads VI, 9): An Analytical Commentary*, Amsterdam: J. C. Gieben.

O'Daly, G. 1973. *Plotinus' Philosophy of the Self,* Irish University Press: Shannon.

O'Meara, Dominic J., 1993. *Plotinus: an Introduction to the Enneads.* Oxford: Oxford University Press.

Pépin, J. 1958. *Mythe et allégorie: les origins grecques et les contestations judéo-chrétiennes.* Paris: Aubier.

Remes, Pauliina. 2007. *Plotinus on Self: The Philosophy of the 'We.'* Cambridge: Cambridge University Press.

———. 2008. *Neoplatonism.* Berkeley: University of California Press.

Rist, John M., 1967. *Plotinus: The Road to Reality.* Cambridge: Cambridge University Press.

Schniewind, Alexandrine. 2003. *L'Éthique du Sage chez Plotin.* Paris: J. Vrin.

Smith, A. 1974. *Porphyry's Place in the Neoplatonic Tradition: A Study in Post-Plotinian Neoplatonism.* The Hague: Nijhoff.

———. 1981. "Potentiality and the Problem of Plurality in the Intelligible," in *Neoplatonism and Early Christian Thought*, eds. H. J. Blumenthal and R. A. Markus. London: Variorum, 99–107.

———. 2004. *Philosophy in Late Antiquity.* London: Routledge.

Theiler, W. 1960. "Plotin zwischen Platon und Stoa," in *Les Sources de Plotin*, Entretiens Fondation Hardt V, Vandoeuvres-Genève: Fondation Hardt, 63–103.

Wallis, R. T. 1995. *Neoplatonism.* 2nd ed. London: Duckworth.

West, M. L. 1966. *Hesiod* Theogony, *Edited with Prolegomena and Commentary.* Oxford: Clarendon Press.

Index of Ancient Authors

Index of Names and Subjects

PRE-SOCRATICS

By Being, It Is: *The Thesis of Parmenides* by Néstor-Luis Cordero

Parmenides and the History of Dialectic: *Three Essays* by Scott Austin

Parmenides, Venerable and Awesome: *Proceedings of the International Symposium* edited by Néstor-Luis Cordero

The Fragments of Parmenides*: A Critical Text with Introduction and Translation, the Ancient Testimonia and a Commentary* by A. H. Coxon. Revised and Expanded Edition edited with new Translations by Richard McKirahan and a new Preface by Malcolm Schofield

The Legacy of Parmenides: *Eleatic Monism and Later Presocratic Thought* by Patricia Curd

The Route of Parmenides: *Revised and Expanded Edition, With a New Introduction, Three Supplemental Essays, and an Essay by Gregory Vlastos* by Alexander P. D. Mourelatos

To Think Like God: *Pythagoras and Parmenides. The Origins of Philosophy.* Scholarly and fully annotated edition by Arnold Hermann

The Illustrated To Think Like God: *Pythagoras and Parmenides. The Origins of Philosophy by* Arnold Hermann with over 200 full color illustrations

Presocratics and Plato: *A Festschrift in Honor of Charles Kahn* edited by Richard Patterson, Vassilis Karasmanis, and Arnold Hermann

PLATO

A Stranger's Knowledge: Statesmanship, Philosophy, and Law in Plato's *Statesman* by Xavier Márquez

God and Forms in Plato by Richard D. Mohr

Image and Paradigm in Plato's *Sophist* by David Ambuel

Interpreting Plato's Dialogues by J. Angelo Corlett

One Book, the Whole Universe: *Plato's* Timaeus *Today* edited by Richard D. Mohr and Barbara M. Sattler

ETHICS

Sentience and Sensibility: *A Conversation about Moral Philosophy* by Matthew R. Silliman

PHILOSOPHICAL FICTION

Pythagorean Crimes by Tefcros Michaelides

The Aristotle Quest: A Dana McCarter Trilogy. Book 1: Black Market Truth by Sharon M. Kaye

AUDIOBOOKS

The Iliad (unabridged) by Stanley Lombardo
The Odyssey (unabridged) by Stanley Lombardo
The Essential Homer by Stanley Lombardo
The Essential Iliad by Stanley Lombardo

FORTHCOMING

Plato in the Empire: Albinus, Maximus, Apuleius. Text, Translation, and Commentary by Ryan C. Fowler

Ennead I.1: What is the Living Being, and What is Man? by Gerard O'Daly

Ennead I.2: On Virtues by Suzanne Stern-Gillet

Ennead I.6: On Beauty by Andrew Smith

Ennead II.4: On Matter by Anthony A. Long

Ennead II.9: Against the Gnostics by Sebastian Ramon Philipp Gertz

Ennead III.7: On Eternity and Time by László Bene

Ennead III.8: On Nature and Contemplation by George Karamanolis

Ennead IV.7: On the Immortality of the Soul by Barrie Fleet

Ennead V.3: On the Knowing Hypostases by Marie-Élise Zovko

Ennead V.8: On Intelligible Beauty by Andrew Smith

Ennead VI.8: On Free Will and the Will of the One by Kevin Corrigan and John D. Turner